Real Estate Investing for Beginners 2026

The Beginner's Roadmap to Buying Your First Investment Property

Julian Ashford

ISBN: 9781807650438

Published by TPSA Publishing

Table of Contents

INTRODUCTION

eal estate investing has been the key to great wealth since time memorial. Many rich people have become that way by learning how to successfully ıvest in real estate. They took the time to learn how to purchase, manage, nd leverage real estate to generate passive cash flow even when they are sleep. They build a strong asset base, which has earned them the right to ecome financially free.

ou can also earn your ticket to financial freedom when you learn how real state investing works. While it is true that real estate is a great investment pportunity, when you lack the wisdom and knowledge about how to operate it, hings might turn sour. The game of real estate involves a lot of capital and rain. If you have the capital without the brain, you will commit financial uicide.

et, a brain without the capital will lead you nowhere. Therefore, you want to earn how real estate investing works and how to raise money to build a strong ıvestment empire. This will start with your mindset, traits, and values. When ou have the mental thought pattern of highly successful real estate investors, ou will be able to weather the storms and do well financially.

deally, you can make money in real estate either through the capital gains ystem or cash flow. When you invest in real estate for capital gains, you buy, x, and sell properties. However, when you invest in cash flow, you invest in uying, holding and collecting rent. The rent will be collected and then used to ay down for other real estate properties while using leverage.

hrough effective property management systems, the value of the property vill be increased over time. This will enable you to pay down the mortgage on he property, decrease your liabilities, increase your equity, and grow your net vorth over time. Using the principles, hacks, and methods of in the following ages, you will be able to multiply your real estate holdings in a short period f time.

CHAPTER ONE: THE BASICS OF REAL ESTATE INVESTING

"Don't wait to buy real estate, buy real estate, and wait."

– T. Harv Eker

'e all started in life by working for money. But, at some point, we began to ealize that working for money is not enough. We began to find ways to earn assive streams of income that doesn't involve so much effort on our part. uckily, some people found that way of life and worked their way to financial idependence.

thers simply struggle through life, working for a paycheck all through their ves. If you're one of those people, looking for a way to start building your assive streams of income, one of the ways you can achieve that dream is real state investing. Through real estate investing, you can build your own nancial powerhouse and achieve financial dreams.

ale Carnegie, one of the most successful businessmen and investors in istory, said, "90% of all millionaires become so through owning real estate." y building and owning your own real estate investing, you can set yourself up or financial freedom. Depending on your vision, relationship, network, and nodel, you can amaze wealth beyond your wildest imagination.

all gets started by your desire and commitment. If you have the burning esire to leverage real estate to create massive wealth, and you have the ommitment to do what it takes to get there, nothing will be impossible for ou. While some people love the game of real estate investing, one of their hallenges is their thinking that real estate investing is very hard and difficult.

Vell, real estate investing is not as hard and difficult as you think. When you rab and understand the basics of real estate investing, you'll realize that real state investing is not complicated. It's very simple. You need to get a solid nderstanding of the foundations of successful real estate investing.

oshua Kennon, co-author of The Complete Idiot's Guide to Investing and nanaging director of Kennon-Green & Co, said, "Real estate investing really an be as conceptually simple as playing monopoly when you understand the asic factors of the investment, economics, and risk. To win, you buy roperties, avoid bankruptcy, and generate rent so that you can buy even nore properties."

Once you understand how real estate investing works, you'll be more equipp to enter the game and succeed. To get started, let's look at what real esta investing is and the nitty grits surrounding it.

What's Real Estate Investing

Even though there are a lot of industry experts who provide a basic definiti of real estate investing, Wikipedia's definition is more extensive. So, you mig want to take a look at what Wikipedia says before getting started with re estate investing. This definition is comprehensive because it takes a holis view and not just one side of it. Let's take a look at it then:

"Real estate investing involves the purchase, ownership, management, rent and/or sale of real estate for profit. Improvement of realty property as part a real estate investment strategy is generally considered to be a sub-specia of real estate investing called real estate development. A real estate is asset form with limited liquidity relative to other investments, it is also capi intensive (although capital may be gained through mortgage leverage) and highly cash flow dependent. If these factors are not well understood a managed by the investor, real estate becomes a risky investment." -Wikiped

When you analyze the definition, you'll notice that the game of real esta investing is a three-fold activity: purchasing, management, and rental/or sa of a real estate property in order to generate profit. As compared with buyi your own home, your objective is not to make a profit. You just want to b your house and live in it. While you might be enjoying some form of utilit you won't be making money from the property unless you rent or sell it someone.

To do well in real estate investing, you have to focus on gaining, developin and enhancing your skills in all three areas: purchasing, managing, a renting/selling of a real estate property. When you buy a property, and you f to manage it well, the property will lose its value quickly and run into losse Also, when you don't get enough rent from the property, you'll not ma enough profit, which will force you to sell it below the right market value.

In a nutshell, we'll say that real estate investing is the purchase, ownershi lease, or sale of land and any structures on it for the purpose of earni money. The real estate properties may include lands, houses, shopping mal hotels, warehouses, resorts, and many others.

Difference between Real Estate Developers and Real Estate Investors

There's a difference between real estate development and real estate investi The first one is usually carried out by real estate developers.

ıe main business of real estate developers is to develop a real estate ·operty for the market. They purchase land, build a house on it, and then ıally sell it to make a profit. Then, they use the profit to build another house ıd on and on. A real estate developer does not care so much about rentals ıd management of a property. They build to sell! That's their game!

ɔmetimes, real estate developers can buy a dilapidated building, renovate, ıd then sell it to the real estate market. They fix homes and then sell them ıck to the market. Whereas real estate developers do these things, they can so take the role of real estate investors. That is to say that a real estate ɛveloper can also double as a real estate investor.

real estate investor is the business of purchasing real estate property, asing it, and make money from rental income. They hold the property for a ɛry long time, while they collect monthly, quarterly or yearly rental income. ·om time to time, they manage and renovate the property to make sure it eets the demands of the tenants.

real estate investor might sell the property after some time, but it will be ased on a lot of factors. This necessarily does not make the real estate vestor a developer. Generally, real estate investor is in the game of buy and ɔld while real estate developers are in the game of build/buy and sell. One cuses on cash flow from rentals, while the latter focuses on cash from capital ains/property sales.

Difference Type of Real Estate Investment Properties

you're looking to be a real estate investor or developer, one of the decisions ɔu have to make is which area to focus on. You need to be really clear about ɔur area of focus in real estate. When you narrow your focus to a selected ɛw of real estate investment property, you'll be in a good position to do well real estate investing over a long period of time.

eal estate investment properties can be categorized into four main areas:

Residential Real Estate

asically, residential real estate involves all types of properties for domestic ses. People rent or buy these properties to live in them, rather than use them s a working area for their business. With that said, a person can rent a house nd create a home office to run a small business; but's still a residential roperty. Some of these residential properties include single-family homes, partments, multi-family homes, condos, and townhouses.

Commercial Real Estate

As the name states, a commercial real estate is rented or bought with t main objective of doing business. The property is used as an office to rur business. Examples of commercial real estate properties are farmlanc shopping malls, offices, rented business lands, restaurants, supermarke banking halls, and large apartment buildings.

Industrial Real Estate

Industrial real estate is rented or purchased by industries or manufacturi companies to be used as warehouses, shipping centers, factories, and pla maintenance centers. All these properties help companies to carry out th production and inventory storage objectives.

Mixed-use Real Estate

These types of real estate properties are commercial, but they are used serve domestic purposes. Examples of mixed-use properties are hotels, gue houses, tourist resorts, and recreational centers. If you own a hotel, it's, fi of all, a commercial property, but your customers might use it as a form o temporary residence as compared to a rented apartment.

5 Ways to Invest in Real Estate

Okay, you have a desire to become a real estate investor. That's good! Bu how do you get started investing in real estate? What are some of the ways investing in real estate? Well, the following are some of the ways to invest ir real estate property:

Active Real Estate Investing

This is where many real estate investors get started. They engage themselv in all the three major roles of real estate investing: buying, managing, a renting a real estate property to make a profit. This is more like a hands- approach to real estate investing, where the real estate investors run t entire show.

A typical real estate investor is the traditional landlord with the ability to g tenants, manage tenants, and renovate the property regularly. T challenging of managing all these critical areas of the real estate property one of the main issues that wears off many landlords. The headaches preve them from scaling their real estate portfolio.

Passive Real Estate Investing

This is the entrepreneurial approach to real estate investing. As entrepreneur engaged in real estate investing, the idea is to form tean roups, and outsourcing agents to handle all the areas related to real estate ıvesting. A passive real estate investor has a turnkey system with a team of xperts that purchase, manage, and runs the property to generate profit. This s a hands-off approach to real estate investing.

'he main work of the passive real estate investor is to seek financing and get he teams to work. He/she must be good at leading and handling teams of eople. Most often, a passive real estate investor will have a real estate nanagement team that will get renters, manage them, and also maintain the roperty. The real estate investor will just collect monthly, quarterly and nnual rental income. However, management expenses and overhead will ave to be paid for all professional expertise.

Real Estate Equity Funds

'his is another type of hands-off approach to real estate investing. In this case, 'ou'll not be directly in control of the investment. Rather, your money will be ised by a real estate investment group to invest in a real estate property vhere you will earn dividends and capital appreciation.

real estate equity fund pools money from the general public to invest in real state properties. They make profits and then distribute the profit earned from nvesting activities to all the shareholders of the equity fund. When you invest n the fund, you'll own a percentage of the earnings or assets of the group.

'here are various types of real estate equity funds:

- ***Real Estate Investment Trusts (REITS):*** They are real estate corporations that pools money from investors to invest in well-diversified real estate properties. They function like dividend-paying stocks and pay off 90% of their annual taxable profits to investors as dividends. At least 75% of their investment and earnings must be in real estate, and they are required to have a management team run the entire operation. REIT registered with SEC are publicly traded.

- ***Opportunity Funds:*** They are funds whose investment capital from investors is used, especially to invest in areas that fall under the opportunity zone program. According to the law, Opportunity Funds must invest at least 90% of their capital in low-income communities and neighborhoods stated under the program. They stand to get amazing tax benefits as they honor the governments' requirements.

- **Private Equity Funds:** They are more like private funds where investor pool money to invest in properties. They are private REIT held by high net worth investors with enough liquidity to invest in real estate properties. These kinds of func are selective and aren't open to the general public.

- ***Online Real Estate Investment Platforms*:** They are onlir investment platforms that pools many from all types of investo and invest it for them in a chosen real estate portfolio, that w under all circumstance, be out of their reach. Rules ar regulations apply in investing through these platforms, and yo have to read more about their track record before investing. Yo can either invest equity or debt. A typical example is Fundrais with over $ 7.5 billion investment.

Online Rental Platforms

Maybe you have a home with a spare bedroom that you might want to rent fo a short period of time. To make money through real estate investing, you ca choose to leverage online rental platforms. These online rental platforr function almost like a hotel and enable you to make money through rentin your spare bedroom for visitors overnight using their platform. You'll b required to furnish and maintain your room for rentals. Rental income will b split between you and the online platform. Airbnb is one of the best onlin rental platforms to use.

Real Estate Trading

Real estate trading takes a different approach from normal real estat investing. When you are in the game of real estate trading, you buy, fix, an sell. Take your property and then invest in another property. By trading an taking your capital quickly, you are able to build your equity over time. challenge with real estate trading is financing and short term ownership of th property.

To be a real estate trader, you need to understand the real estate market. Yo have to know when the market is experiencing a bull or bear condition. Whe the market falls, and prices of real estate properties are going down, you'll b forced to sell your properties below their market value cash flow real estat investors. Beware of the real estate bubble when flipping houses or any kind c real estate.

5 Ways to Make Money in Real Estate

There are various ways of making money in real estate. This makes real estat an attractive investment for many people looking to diversify their portfolic Once you understand how money is made in real estate, you can simpl choose your way of investing in real to make money.

1. *Appreciation*: When the value of your real estate property increased, you can sell and make more money. Usually, property appreciation comes with property management and the area within which the real estate property resides. When the area improves, the value of the property in the area also increases.

2. *Rental income*: You get to collect rents from tenants who reside in your property. The thrill of monthly rental income is what persuades and drives many people to invest in real estate properties. Rental income provides stable cash flow to maintain, enhance the property, and take care of the landlord.

3. *Phantom Income*: Owing a real estate investment comes with special tax breaks that provide a form of income. When you get huge tax savings from the government, you can use that savings to buy more properties or invest in improving existing properties.

4. *Ancillary income*: Many real estate investors create another form of revenue streams that generate money from the property. For example, vending machines or laundry services provide a source of income for real estate investors.

The Risks of Real Estate Investing

If you're going to be a successful real estate investor, you need to understand what the odds are. If you're not well informed about the risks regarding real estate investing, you'll lose a lot of money. Many people naively say that real estate investing is safe, profitable, and stable.

Just like all investing activities, there are risks involved. And there are risks involved in real estate investing. Each property you own has its own risks. If you don't manage the risks well, you'll run into losses that will force you to sell the property below its market value.

So then, what are the risks of real estate investing?

Highly Priced Properties

This is the first and most fundamental area of risk in real estate investing. Take note; we're focused on real estate investing, not development. When you buy properties at a very high cost, it might be very hard for the rental income and all other ancillary income sources to cover costs over time. And this is one of the risks.

High Management Expenses

High management or operational expenses is another key area of real estate investing. If your costs of managing and running the real estate are higher than the money from it, then you'll actually be going to get in troub financially. This is one of the major risks of real estate investing, and the ma reason you have to analyze costs very well before buying a property.

Low Rental Income

Sometimes, you might not even get renters to rent. It might also be that yo rent is so high that people within the catchment area of the property arer able to afford it. It might even be that your property is not rented to fu capacity, and that is leading to low income.

Inability to Cover Mortgage Payments

If you use leverage through mortgage financing, you'll have to cover the cos of the mortgage through the property. But, if your rental income is not enoug to cover the mortgage payment of the property, then you'll be in big troub financially. The banks or the financial institutions will be forced to take ov the property and sell it to get their money invested in the underlying property

CHAPTER TWO: WHY SHOULD YOU BECOME A REAL ESTATE INVESTOR

"Real estate investing offers many advantages, and investors can enjoy a steady income flow that may lead to financial freedom."

- Benilyn Formoso

al estate investing is the gateway to financial freedom. Even when you've ilt a successful business that runs with or without you, the free cash flow nerated by the business must still be invested in income-generating assets. e cash flow generated by the business must be invested to increase your set base and grow the business.

ually, big businesses expand through acquisitions. They acquire other sinesses and grow their portfolio of businesses. Apart from growing your sets through acquisitions, you can also invest your free cash flow into an come-generating real estate that produces passive cash flow. As you do this er a period of time, you'd realize that your network will be increasing.

hile real estate is not the only way to achieve financial freedom, investing in al estate will give you a better diversification and flexibility. You'll get to arn a lot about debt, financing, managing, people, human behavior, and any others. The experience gained can be used to enhance your business, reer and professional life.

you're looking to invest in real estate, but have been wondering what the nefits of real estate investing will be, the following are some mind-blowing sights to get you off the ideation stage to the execution stage, where you're tively working on your goals:

Equity Building

sically, there are three types of money: income, profit, and equity. Most ten, people's mind is fixated on the income statement, so all they think out is more income and more profit. But, equity is more important than come and profit. The goal of an investment manager is to increase the equity the total investment portfolio through increasing income and profit.

ow, there's something special about real estate investing. Since real estate operties are usually highly expensive, most investors can't pay upfront. This ads to debt financing for traditional banks, private lenders, and so forth. If a)% down payment has been used to buy a rental house followed by 80%

leverage, from a bank, it will mean that the original investor's equity is 20
Leverage attracts interest and other tactical requirements.

To increase the equity of the investor, the loan/leverage must be p regularly. April Kozlowski Palomino said, "As you pay off your mortgage, y build equity. As you build equity, you now have the leverage to acqu additional rental properties and increase your cash flow."

As the property makes income and part of the profit is used to pay mortgage and loans, the liability/leverage/loan on the property reduces, a the equity of the owner increases. After a period of time, all the debts will paid, and the investor will own the underlying property 100%. This is ultimate goal of a real estate investor.

Building Passive Income

There are three types of income: ordinary income, capital gains, and pass income. 90% of the world's population has been trained to make their mor through the ordinary income loop. When you make most of your mor through this channel, you'll also be taxed the most. To receive tax benef you need to find mediums of making money through capital gains and pass income.

Thanks to real estate investing, you can start earning passive income. Wha a passive income? Its money that you earn regular income without having work hard all the time for it. You work hard once, and the money kee coming, with little or no little maintenance to the revenue stream. Real est can help you generate a passive income that will lead to financial freedom.

What's financial freedom? It's when your income exceeds your mont expenses. That means when the monthly passive income exceeds yo monthly expenses, you'll be financially free. As simple as that. To maint your lifestyle, you just have to increase your passive cash flow from the r estate properties.

"Your rental properties will work for you even when you are sleeping. buying several rental properties that generate enough income to cover yo expenses, you have the freedom to do what you enjoy, instead of spending of your time at work," says Braddy Hanna, chief executive officer of Mill Cre Home Buyers. This is why many rich people love using real estate investing generate passive income to grow their wealth.

Cash Flow for Retirement

Many corporate executives and professionals have already realized that t cash flow from their retirement is not enough for a pension. In view of th they have decided to start investing in real estate. There are ma overnment works and corporate executives, building their own portfolio of eal estate and generating passive income for their retirement.

Vhen you take your time to invest in real estate, the passive income source om the property will serve as a supplement for your 401(K) and many others. any old people worry that their monthly pension income will not be enough o cater for their living expenses. Instead of worrying, you can start investing our surplus money into real estate.

he best approach here is not real estate trading. Flipping will not serve well hen it comes to creating cash flow for retirement. You can use real estate quity, passive real estate investing, or active real estate investing to achieve our goal. If you do the math and plan everything well, your passive cash flow vill provide a great source of revenue for you during your older days.

Hedging Against Inflation

lot of people say that cash is king. But cash can become worth less than its alue with increasing inflation. When inflation is growing at a steady rate, nany people begin to get afraid. Their savings and cash at the bank begin to ose value as the purchasing power of their money goes down. Well, if you've nvested much of your money in real estate, you don't have to worry too much.

he exciting thing about inflation is that it causes the value of a real estate roperty to increase. The more information goes high, the more rental income ncreases. That means making more money with the same property. This also auses the property to appreciate in value. It serves a cushion and protects ne property against depreciation due to inflation.

herefore, real estate investing becomes a sure bet against inflation. A recent eport indicated that "the average annual real estate appreciation rate ationwide has been nearly 6 per cent in recent decades, while the inflation ate rarely reaches 4 per cent." Inflation will work for you as opposed to vorking against your plan to raise money.

uring the time of inflation, you don't buy real estate properties. You simply old and let the value of your property compound over time. When the market oes down, you will just have to buy a lot of real estate properties at the owest price possible.

Unlimited Tax Benefits

One exciting reason to be a real estate investor is to make money through apital gains and passive income. Passive income from real estate is tithed ifferent from ordinary income from your physical efforts. The key to financial uccess is not ordinary income.

You'll have to find a way to convert your ordinary income into passive a portfolio income. Apart from the fact that ordinary income is taxed higher, t government also withdraws the taxes before you even get paid. That mea you paid taxes before even getting your money. This is not the same investing in real estate.

Due to the nature of real estate investing, it's advisable that you inve through a corporation. To get the tax benefits that a real estate provides, y have to use a limited liability corporate structure to shield your real esta property. Through a corporation, you can make your expenses for the re estate before you even pay the taxes on it.

If you get a corporate attorney and make him part of your team, you can able to find real estate tax loopholes that will help you shield and grow yo wealth. Investing in real estate through a corporation also prevents yo personal assets from terrible lawsuits that can wipe you out.

Leverage for Financing

Real estate properties are very expensive and require a lot of money purchase. It's very hard to build an extensive real estate portfolio witho having to access to financing. To expand your real estate portfolio, you c either use debt or equity. Whichever financing instrument you use will he you achieve your goal, but every one of them has its own advantages.

When you are into real estate, you can be able to use the leverage fro traditional banks to grow. That's to say that you can use the banker's mon to become rich. With a 20% down payment, you can get a traditional lo from financial institutions to buy more properties. As you gain mo experience and track record in real estate investing, you can get 100 financing with 0% equity down payment from your pocket.

As you pay the mortgage on the property, you'll eventually pay off the lo and finally own the property 100%. So, what's the catch? Real estate enabl you to use good debt to make more money than you ever dreamed possible. enables you to other people's money (OPM) to generate passive income ar become rich.

Cash Flow for Lifestyle

Robert Kiyosaki said, "Assets buy luxuries." The rich invest first and then th passive income from their investment provides their real estate In effect, th still own the investment, but the investment is making them afford the bett life without having to work hard for the money that acquired the liabilities su as luxury cars.

ıvesting a real estate is your ticket to living a better life. You can use cash ɔw from your real estate to improve your standard of living. You can even ngage in philanthropy and give back to society. When you engage in acts of nilanthropy, the community benefits from your wealth and gives you prestige nd honor for your achievement.

ɔu can also use real estate as an investment vehicle to finance your child's ɔllege education. If you've successful bought income-generating real estate ır your children, the cash flow from the real estate will pay for their lifestyle nd college tuition fees. You still own the real estate, but the monthly cash ɔw the property will take care of your child's lifestyle.

hat's why Marc A. Van Steyn said, "Real estate investing can be an lternative vehicle for college savings. It is recommended that young families ıvest in the purchase of one property for each child they believe will attend ɔllege. The property can be financed with a 15-year mortgage, thus being aid off prior to the child's 18th birthday. It allows families to actively save ırough the renters' payments. When the property is paid off, they can either ell or continue to use it as a source of cash flow.

Final Thoughts

you've been hoping to start investing in real estate, this is the time. Don't ait. Even if you don't have enough money to invest in real estate, you can do indirectly through real estate investment trusts (REITs). You can start ıvesting in real estate and get the incredible benefits of investing in real state. After you have learned, gained the knowledge and courage to get tarted, you can start investing by yourself using any of the real estate ıvestment models.

ꞆHAPTER THREE: THE MINDSET OF SUCCESSFUL REAL ESTATE INVESTORS

"Real estate cannot be lost or stolen, nor can it be carried away. Purchased with common sense, paid for in full and managed with reasonable care, it is about the safest investment in the world."

– Franklin D. Rosevelt

ny idiot can buy a real estate as long as the money is available. But the ıallenge is converting the real estate property into an income-generating ;set that pays the mortgage and acquires other assets. Turning a property to a money-making making machine requires a specific mindset.

l successful real estate investors know how to play the game. They have an visible thinking process that they go through before they purchase, manage, ıd generate rental income from any real estate. In reality, the secret of their ıccess is not because of their investment skills and techniques. It's actually ıe to their mindset—the mental thought pattern—of taking the trash and turn into cash.

sk any super successful real estate investor on how they made, and it, and ıey will tell you this: they buy mediocre properties from mediocre real estate vestors and then leverage their mindset to convert the mediocre asset into a eat asset that produces a steady flow of income. This is why developing the ght mindset is crucial for successful real estate investing.

ccording to the Pareto Principle, 80% of the success is achieved by 20% of ıe very best people. This same thing also works in the real estate market. In al estate, it is not how educated or smart you are, at the end of the day, eople want to know if you know how to use leverage to buy, manage and andle real estate properties that create passive cash flow.

aving the mindset of successful real estate investors is a prerequisite for ıccess. If you're going to be successful in real estate investing, it is cumbent on you to study people who have made it before you and learn how ıey think, behave act. The way upward is to learn from people who have ade it and then follow their footsteps with intelligence.

'hen you think, behave and act in the saw way like successful real estate ıvestors, you'll be successful. You see, success leaves clues. Success can be odeled and imitated. You don't have to reinvent the wheel, by imitating the excellence of others, you can speed up your rate of achieving your goals a become the best of who you are.

Your mindset is a set of beliefs and thoughts that you habitually allow occupy your mind. When you believe something to be true and have eviden to back it up, you'll gain the confidence to work on it. In the same mann when you have the right beliefs, knowledge, and ideas about real est investing, you become very confident in your operations.

The Right Mindset for Successful Real Estate Investing

Just having the money alone will not make you successful in real estate. Y need to ensure that you have the right mindset to convert the money into asset that provides consistent cash flow. So, which type of mindset do y need to have to be successful in real estate investing?

Long Term Perspective

For people who want to make a quick profit, real estate is not for you. you're going to make money in real estate, you have to approach it with long term mentality. If you're looking to make money quickly and faster in t market, then you need to try something else. It takes time to buy, manag and start generating rental income from real estate.

Most mortgage financing for real estate properties takes between ten to fi years, depending on the terms of operation. If you have used a mortgage finance your real estate and you're required to pay back in twenty years, it w mean that the property must be paying monthly mortgage for twenty yea before you finally own the property 100%. That requires a long term approac

However, if you want to make money quickly, you can consider flipping re estate. Instead of buying and holding properties to collect rents, you can foc on selling to take a property. However, that's not the main approach successful real estate investors. Notwithstanding, you can choose th approach to real estate investing if you don't want to hold properties a collect rents.

Having a long term perspective requires you to have the vision to add value the properties in your portfolio. You need to have a systemic plan to improv renovate and creatively manage the properties under your care so that th value compounds over time. You can consider adding bedrooms, garage, offi space, and many others just to increase value and make money.

Continuous Learning

People who are not addicted to learning might not do well in real estate. T real estate market is always changing rapidly, and you can lose your value a redibility. The way to stay relevant to the field is to engage in continuous earning. You need to have a plan in place that ensures you acquire the ecessary education, skills, and techniques required to be successful in real state.

he most successful real estate investors have in-depth information about neir field. They have studied longer than their competitors; therefore, they lso know much more than their competitors. And you see, in this modern rea, knowledge is a great source of competitive advantage. If someone nows better than you, they'll also do better than you.

nd this is the reason you need to be hungry for information about real estate nvesting. You need to listen, watch, and read the news. You have to study the eal estate market to the extent that you can accurately predict the direction nd the movement of the market before it even moves. When you understand he market and the dynamics, it put you in the position to attract better pportunities to be successful.

f you want to get started in real estate investing, and you're wondering what ou should learn about, the following should be your starting point: how to alue a property, how to analyze the market, how to find the economic drivers f the market, how to manage a property, how to hire and fire people, how to andle people's emotions, how to raise money, how to manage cash flow roperly and many others.

Laser Focus Mindset

ocus is critical for success in real estate. If you want to make it in real estate, hen you have to develop the ability to focus. There're many problems and bstacles in real estate, which requires you to have a stubborn persistence oupled with the focus to stay on until your goal has been achieved. In view of his, you might want to develop this single trait.

ne of the reasons a lot of people are not successful in their careers is due to lack of focus. They put their attention on many things that don't work at all. Vhen they get into the game of real estate, they trade and invest in various narkets that do not profit well. As a result, much of their capital is locked up n real estate, and they never get ahead.

he key to success is to focus on those few things that generate the best esult. And how do you know them? Use the Pareto principle to find out the op 20% of your real estate investments that produce 80% of the result. nstead of doing many things, you focus on only the top 20%. As a result, ou'll produce better results than the average real estate investor will down.

he key is to narrow your focus and learn to overcome obstacles. Set goals nd decide on how many properties you want to acquire each year. Once you have decided that, stay focus on the number until it is achieved. Whe problems come on the way, deal with them, and focus on your goal. When yo develop the habit of setting and achieving your goals through the power focus, you'll become successful.

Relationship Building

You've heard this saying before, "Your net worth is your network." In th business of real estate, the power of a network cannot be underestimated. Yo have to consciously build and develop the right relationships that will enhan your investments. Always remember that it takes a team to make a drea work. To achieving your real estate investing dream, you can't do it all b yourself.

From placing bids, winning bids, obtaining permits, securing loans, handlin customers, placing advertisements, approving renovations, and all others, yo need the right people to work with. This does not necessarily mean that yo should employ people. Only employ the right resources when it is needed. Bu the keys are to start building the right network and maintaining them in peaceful way to ensure the success of your real estate investing activities.

People revolve around real estate properties. That means a real estate serve a link for people to connect and build thriving relationships. For example, you own a hotel in town, your hotel can serve as a medium to connect wit other successful people who might visit your hotel. You will intend to leverag that relationship to achieve the results you want.

Sales, marketing, communication, deal-making, and negotiation skills ar critical for building relationships. Take courses and read books that wi enhance your communication skills. Aside from this, you have to ensure yo model integrity, trust, and honesty in all your business relationships. Whe people realize that you're not the type that keeps your word, they will fail t trust and not do business with you. This will not only affect your reputation bu also your balance sheet.

Leveraging Resources

The game of real estate is the game of leverage. If you don't know how to us leverage to grow your real estate portfolio, you can't achieve much. But whe you master the art of using leverage, you'll be able to accumulate a lot o income-producing real estates in a short period of time. It's virtuall impossible to achieve something big in real estate if you're going to rely o your own savings.

How many real estates can you buy with your own savings? And how man days and years will it take you to save money to buy ten real estate propertie o play the game of real estate, you need to understand money and how to everage other people's money to acquire more assets. When mastering the rt of using other people's money (OPM), you'll position yourself for xtraordinary wealth.

he exciting part of using leverage in real estate is that you'll be providing alue to your investors/creditors through interest and dividend payments. You re not only providing housing and properties for the community, but you are lso making people rich. The more you buy properties and pay back earnings the required party, the more you grow your portfolio.

is not only money that must be leveraged to scale, but other people's time nd resources. You need to know how to hire and put smart people to work. Vhen you learn the art of leadership and use teams to run your real estate usiness, you can be able to grow and increase your real estate portfolio over period of time.

Maximizing Opportunities

ou need to also learn how to take advantage of opportunities. The key to uccess in real estate investing is to maximize the opportunities at disposal nd get the best result from it. Success breeds success. As you succeed at one hing, it opens a door for another. Instead of becoming complacent, you need o leverage your success to keep moving forward. When you make a mistake nd fail, you need to learn from those mistakes and take the next step of ction that will lead you to the next level.

omeone said, "Success is when opportunity meets preparation." When you vork on yourself, plan, and project, you'll begin to attract the opportunities hat will enable you to make money in the real estate market over a period of ime. You need to be optimistic and see the best in every problem. Instead of ooking at the problem, look at the opportunity to be realized.

eal estate responds to market conditions. When the right market indicators re in place, you will be able to get as many renters as possible for your roperty. When you see an environment in trouble, you have two main choices: ou can choose to look at the problem, but you can also choose to look at the pportunity that will be realized when you solve the problem.

Jnfortunately, many people look at the problem, so they never invest. Success eal estate investors are always looking for opportunities. They are looking for n opportunity to invest, raise money, get more tenants, reduce operational osts, renovate, and increase the value of their property. When you begin to ealize these things, your mind will be tuned to see opportunities that will rant you more doors for success.

Commitment to winning

Commitment is crucial for success in real estate investing. Many things ca happen in the course of your handling real estate deals. You need to have th strength of character to stay on guard until success shows up. You need develop the self-discipline to keep going when the going gets tough and har That requires a commitment to winning at all costs.

Are you committed to winning? Do you the courage to handle projects eve when things are not going your way? Many people simply give up when thin get tough. They fail to commit to winning and persevere when the econom winds turn against them. If you're going to be successful in real esta investing, then being strong, courageous, and fighting hard is crucial.

When you are committed to winning, you remain calm and patient when time are tough. Instead of complaining and murmuring, you focus your energies o how to maximize the mistakes to your advantage. This will enable you overcome the challenges you are facing and breakthrough. You need understand the difference between process and result. While you need to focu on results, you need to commit to the process to get the required result.

Successful real estate investor, David Greene said, "The best investors hav learned to temper this pressure with wisdom and patience. They know whe they need to run fast, and when they need to stop and wait to see how thin develop. Patience can take several forms when it comes to real esta investing. Learning to recognize areas where you'll need to practice it can sav you from a lot of expensive mistakes." Stay committed to the process, not th result.

CHAPTER FOUR: HOW TO FIND REAL ESTATE INVESTMENT PROPERTIES

"90% of all Millionaires become so through owning real estate. More money has been made in real estate than all industrial investments combined. The wise young man or wage earner of today invests his money in real estate."

—Andrew Carnegie

e benefits of investing in real estate are overwhelming. While the stock arket can swing left and right and go bust occasions, the real estate market fairly stable. That is to say that the inherent value in a real estate property u own will still be available even when the market prices have dropped down ittle bit. This makes real estate the flavor of the rich.

his book, Rich Dad Poor Dad, Robert Kiyosaki stated that his rich dad told n that the secret to becoming rich is to buy assets, not liabilities. What's an set? An asset is anything that puts money into your pocket. Whereas an set puts money into your pocket, liabilities take money out of your pocket. If u're going to be successful in finding the right real estate investment operties, you have to have these definitions in mind.

hy? If you don't buy an income-producing real estate, you're not going to ake any money investing in real estate. A real estate can actually become a bility when it takes money out of your pocket more than it makes you. This why you have to be careful when looking for a real estate property. You ant to look for an asset that will appreciate over time and produce regular sh flow.

the flip side, finding a real estate investment property is not easy. There's lot of working and skills required to find a good real estate investment operty. The first step is to look for many options and choose from then. metimes, a key way to help find good real estate investment properties is ur strategy.

r instance, if your strategy involves buying, fixing, and selling properties, an what you need is to search for real estates that are not in good condition d buy them lower than their market prices. You need to have criteria or eck for selecting what best fits your strategy. After you purchase the operty, you simply have to fix and then sell it back to the market.

However, if your strategy involves buying and renting out, you need to hav yardstick for selecting the right real estate property. In this case, you mi buy a worn our real estate, fix and rent or simply buy one with little issues a then put it back to the market place. The plan is to find a real estate prope that meets your plan, objective, and investing strategy.

Where to Find Real Estate Investment Properties

If you're looking to purchase good real estate investment properties, ther couple of places you have to turn to. You need to have a clear idea of wh you want so that you can easily pick out and select what fits your nee Nonetheless, the following places can serve as a good start for finding go real estate investment properties.

Real Estate Network

The importance of building your network cannot be underestimated. Yo network can be a valuable source of assistance when you are looking to b real estate. You see, building your network is more like signing up for insurance policy and paying your monthly premiums. You never know wh disaster will strike. You just keep paying your premium until one day when accident happens.

At that time, you simply call your insurance broker to process a claim for yo issue. Since you've been faithful in keeping the terms of the policy, insurance company will take care of all the charges related to the accident t has happened. In that way, the insurance premium will actually pay off. Tha the same way building a network works in real estate.

You need to be active and be intentional in building your network. If you're the game of real estate, it is very important that you build a stro relationship network. It's through your relationship that you will be able to some of the most prestigious and profitable real estate properties. T network you will build today will work for you in building your net wo tomorrow.

So, what do you do to build your network? Here're a few suggestions:

- Join a real estate owner's association in your city/town community.
- Join real estate investment clubs in your city/town/commun
- Make friends with other real estate investors in yo city/town/community.
- Attend real estate investing conferences/seminars a workshops.

- **Reach out to help other real estate investors in one way or another.**
  - Build a relationship with professionals such as realtors accountants, attorneys, realtors that work for real estate owners/investors.
  - Build a good relationship with bankers that deal with real estate related activities.
  - Contact property managers in your city/town or community and tell them of your needs.
  - Make friends with politicians and city officials that deal with the selling of real estate properties
  - Let your family, relatives, and friends know that you're into real estate investing.
  - Let your church or any social association you belong to know that you're into real estate investing.
  - Provide social responsibility to your community under the name of your real estate company.
- **Join meetups and online groups that deal with real estate investing activities.**

here's no one single way to building your network, and you can't say that ou've got enough network, so there's no need to keep building it. No! You ave to understand that some of the opportunities you need tomorrow will be atered for by the network you have today. You have to constantly be building our network for the future. That's the key to success in real estate investing.

Real Estate Brokers/Agent

ou need to see real estate brokers/agents as your eyes in the market. When ou have good brokers, they will make you money by bringing you good real state properties with incredible financing opportunities that will make you uccessful in the long run. A good broker should be more like an advisor, ounselor and guide to buying high-quality real estate properties.

lany solo real estate investors want to do it all by themselves. Therefore, ney don't see the need to buy real estate properties. They think that using a roker or agent to buy a real estate property will be a lot of hassle. They want o save money by doing the job of searching for the real estate market. Thus, ney are not able to scale their real estate investment portfolio.

Even if you're the solo type, you have to learn to leverage real estate broke and agents to find good real estate properties. You see, successful real esta investors don't become successful because they want to micromanage eve step of their real estate investment. They leverage brokers and agents to he them find good real estates, and that saves them time to do other things.

Instead of using all your time to actively search for properties, you ca leverage the expertise of a real estate broker who is always in the market. real estate broker has a wealth of experience, understanding, and knowled about the real estate market. They know the prices of real estate and how process all the buying arrangements. With their support and guidance, you ca buy good properties.

The challenge is finding good real estate agents/brokers. They are some re estate brokers who are just there to make money for themselves. They s your property without looking at the financials and the economics of t property. That's why you need to put in enough time into selecting a choosing the right broker. If you have a good broker, everything will see easy!

So, how do you find a good broker?

- Ask your network for recommendation
- Check their track records and accomplishments
- Focus on their integrity more than their credentials
- Check whether the realtor offers the kind of property yo need.
- **Ensure that you and the realtor are at the same pace when it comes to money.**
- Interview as many real estate agents as possible and sele the one which best fits you.
- **Look for testimonials and other information provided by real estate investors.**

With the help of a good real estate broker, you can be able to get an eli property that will multiply your network over a short period of time. Your re estate broker will work as your partner and help find properties that meet yo investing strategies and objectives.

Real Estate Websites

you're looking for real estate properties, the opportunities are boundless. ay in day out, many property owners want to sell their estates and make oney. There are some people who have inherited properties that they want sell out. For some people, their job demands to move to another country nd work, meaning they have to sell their current property. Divorce and paration also lead to the selling of some vital and valuable real estate roperties.

any of these people get overwhelmed by their situation. They are usually dividual real estate owners who are looking to sell their properties and move n to the next phase of life. Most of them don't even know what to do or how go about selling their real estate properties. To make things simple and asy, they use real estate websites to look for potential buyers.

he real estate websites might decide to charge them something small for sting or selling their property through their platform. This is often to weed out cammers who might be using the site for their dubious activities. The real state websites will often provide detailed descriptions about the property. mong others, the following information will be provided: the price, cap rate, eighborhood, location, size of the property, current status of the property, nd many more.

ome of the most popular websites known for making real estate listing clude the following:

- *Craigslist.org*: They help you to place bids for real estate in a certain location and also look for real estate properties that have been placed by real estate owners and realtors.
- *Auction.com*: They deal with all kinds of bidding related to residential properties. If you're looking to buy houses, fix them up and rent to the market, looking through this place is really great.
- *Trulia App*: This is simply an app that gets you closer to the market and helps you to find local real estate properties that have been listed by their individual owners in your local area. You can download this app from Google Play Store or Apple Store.
- *Loop Net*: If you're focused on looking for commercial properties to boost your real estate portfolio, regularly checking and placing bids on this site is very important.
- *Local Websites*: Look for local community based real estate websites in your area. These websites provide a listing of local

properties, and you can be able to find the property that best f your needs in the right area or locality.

Searching for properties on the real estate website is not a one-way affair. Y need to be focused and consistent in searching to find something good. Ju placing your bid on the website and then waiting for miracles to happen v not happen. You have to consider following up since other real estate investc might also be looking at the property. Use contact numbers that will make easy for sellers to reach or get to you.

You need to be careful when looking for deals through any property. Ju because something looks good online does not mean you should make buy Before you buy any property that has been listed on any real estate websit ensure you have investigated and looked at the property carefully. Inspect t team with a qualified real estate inspection team. Save yourself a lot of hass by doing the due diligence.

Real Estate Platforms

The internet is replete with countless opportunities to get what you wa Literally speaking, you can leverage online platforms like Google, Forums, a Groups to find good real estate properties. The idea here is to advertis Instead of going out there to do the work of searching, you can pay some fe dollars for online advertising platforms to get the job done for you.

While Facebook and LinkedIn are good social media platforms, they are n ideal for looking for real estate properties. What you want to do is to ma sure you leverage digital platforms that have a high sensitivity for real estat and you might easily get a deal there. These platforms have a lot of peop looking to sell or buy real estate properties.

You need to first of all advertising in real estate forums. Look for local re estate forums with buyers and sellers. Some of these platforms place ads their columns, which someone might see and react to. In some cases, y might not even place an ad that you want to buy a house or ant property. T buyers will themselves place ads on the platform which you can quick respond to and buy the property.

While Google might not be your typical real estate platform, you can use it buy properties. First of all, you can use the search bar to look for houses any particular area. For instance, if you're looking for a house in Costa Ric you can simply type "Single-family homes in Costarica for sale." You'll find lot of search results from which you can look at.

Apart from using the search bar, you can place Google Ads. Using Pay-Pe Click Ads, you can be able to find a lot of people contact you for houses th are selling. This will make the job of searching very easy and fun. You simp ave to go and look at what they are offering and see whether it meets your eeds and criteria.

you have a friend who has an email list of real estate audience, you consider veraging that too. If he or she has a database of 1,000 real estate audience, id an email has been fired to them about buying any specific real estate that ey might want to sell, you can be shocked at the response you will get. hile this might be unusual, the deals you will get will not be available in the arket. You might get better real estate deals, which will enhance your ortfolio.

Real Estate Neighborhood Hunt

ne of the most overlooked ways to find real estate properties is to take a jog, alk, or ride in the community you might be looking to buy a real estate operty. If you want to buy a good real estate, you need to have a fair idea of ow the community looks like. If you walk through the community regularly, ou can instinctively know whether the community is a good fit for your real state investment.

hile you walk through the community, you can look at other properties there id figure out how they are priced, sold, and rented. By doing so, you can also id real estate properties that are for sale by their owners. This strategy has elped many real estate investors to find better deals which have not even be ut in the market yet.

ou need to spend some time driving through the neighborhood slowly and equently. As you drive through the neighborhood, you need to pay attention id be hungry, looking for real estate deals that might be available. Your only ost will be your gas and time, but it will be worth it, even if you have not und any kind of property you're looking for. The lessons and things you see ill trigger something and cause you to find properties in the market.

hich kind of properties should you be looking for as you drive through the eighborhood? You look for distressed properties, neglected properties, roperties with for sale signs, troubled rental properties, and poorly managed eal estates. With good management skills, you can buy these properties at a wer rate and then rent it or sell at a higher rate to the market.

Real Estate Magazines & Newspapers

you're a real estate investor, then subscribing to local newspapers and agazines that deal with the real state is crucial. Instead of reading through agazines and newspapers that are not related to what you are doing, you an consider spending time and money on what will help you achieve your goals. Some of these magazines/newspapers provide deals that you'll shocked at.

Instead of just skimming through the magazine or newspaper, consic checking the real estate column and look at the deals that are available. Re through the descriptions provide and look at other related properties there You should not be in haste when looking at these properties. And don't ju believe it because it's in the papers.

You should make a habit of reading through the real estate properties in t newspapers and magazines from time to time. Contact their respective owne and ask for an appointment to look at the underlying property. As usual, y should ensure that you are inspecting the property with a qualified team. Th will ensure that you look at the details surrounding the property.

Use Multiple Ways

There's no single way. What you have to do is to use all the steps provide You never know which will work. Build your network, get in touch with a go real estate broker/agent, find deals on real estate websites, place bids online platforms, and drive through the neighborhood.

By being consistent and steady in your search, you will food a good real esta property that will fetch you a robust cash flow over a period of time.

CHAPTER FIVE: HOW TO ANALYZE REAL ESTATE INVESTMENTS

"Most people think buying is investing, but they're wrong [it] doesn't make you an investor any more than buying groceries makes you a chef."

—Gary Keller

Real estate might be one of the best investments a person can make. But if you not done well, real estate investment can make you bankrupt faster than you think. This is the reason why you need to understand the basics of buying and running a real estate investment property. If you take things lightly and refuse to pay attention to details, you might be in serious trouble.

When it comes to real estate investing, an area most people easily neglect or forget is analyzing the real estate investment property before purchasing. Most people make a mistake, thinking that buying a real estate property makes them a real estate investor. No! Just because you purchase a real estate property does not make you a real estate investor.

There're a lot of things that come in when you're investing in real estate. That's why Gary Keller, one of the most successful real estate investors, said, *"Most people think buying is investing, but they're wrong [it] doesn't make you an investor any more than buying groceries makes you a chef."* To invest in real estate, you need to take a different approach from the usual buying of real estate.

You've got to understand that the purpose of investing is to multiply cash flow and increase net worth. You want to lay some money down today and receive much more in the future. This is not the same as buying a piece of land and holding it for the appreciation for selling it. Your cash can burn when the real estate sector is experiencing a bull market.

While it is important to look for real estate investments, you need to always analyze the property before you buy it. The problem with many beginner investors is that they are too much to become real estate investors that they forget to analyze the property very well before they purchase it. As a result, they make terrible mistakes that force them to sell the property at a premature time.

Golden Rules for Real Estate Analyzing

Are you looking for a real estate property to buy? Are checking with real estat brokers or property managers to buy a property? Whichever medium you ar using to look for and buy the property, you need to know that you cannot sk the process of analyzing the property before purchasing. The following are th rules you must keep in mind for analyzing an investment property:

Don't Believe What Someone Told You

Too often, many amateur real estate investors fall for the sales gimmicks c greedy real estate brokers who are just looking for a way to earn commission. They believe their real estate broker to the extent that the forget to do their homework. Just because a real estate property broker c agent tells you that a property is good does mean you should but it.

You have to forget what is being said and do your own analysis. Conduct you own independent analysis of the property with an independent team of expert Get the facts, the *real* facts, not the *assumed* facts. Always try as much a possible to get first-hand information about the property before releasin funds for payments, to avoid plunging yourself in a problem. Don't fall fc tricks and "tax breaks" gimmicks.

Research and Investigate Thoroughly Before You Invest

This is the key to buying good investment properties. You have to do your du diligence. Once you have bypassed what realtors tell you, then dig in. Whe you do your homework, you will end up buying the property at a good price c not buying it at all. Your research should start by comparing other real estat prices in the area.

Buying a property at high cost is the first recipe for disaster all real estat investors must avoid. Consider looking at rental rates, economic conditions the net operating income, and the vacancy rates of the property. Factc maintenance costs, mortgage payments, and property taxes as well. Researc and get all the details surrounding the property.

Don't Fall in Love with the Investment Property

This is a big trap but falls in it. Many real estate investors tend to fall in lov with the property to the extent that they forget that they aren't buying th property to live in it. Your game as a real estate investor is to buy a propert at the lowest price as possible, rent at the highest price possible and make th highest return as possible from the property.

Falling in love with a property because it is nice and beautiful when it doesn have the economics to make it a good investment is simply a recipe fc isaster. You have forgotten about your feelings about the property and do the omework. Fall in love with the property only if it has great economics and ash flow potential aside being nice.

Ensure All Legal Arrangements Have Been Done

eal estate is a mental game. You need to understand all contracts involving n the contract. You need to know and understand the tenancy lease contract, he real estate purchasing contract, the land contract, the mortgage contract, nd any kind of contract related to the property you're interested in buying. now the terms and conditions involved before signing.

t makes sense to work with a trusted and licensed real estate attorney in nalyzing real estate investments. Your real estate lawyer will help you nderstand and process all documents well before endorsing and signing them. his will help avoid future problems that might come.

Metrics to Look for when Analyzing an Investment Property

Once you observe these golden rules of real estate analysis, you need to look or some key metrics that make a property a good investment. When you nvestigate and examine the property, seeing that everything looks good, you an proceed with the investment. This will ensure that you avoid and reduce isks that might come along with ownership of the property.

he following are some very important metrics to consider before investing in roperty:

The Economics of the Community

Most people say that real estate is a good investment. But the investment is nly as good as the community it resides. When a real estate is a bad ommunity with no jobs, no economic growth, poor social amenities, and all thers, it will have a low value. When the community is not doing well, the eal estate property will decrease in value. But its value will appreciate when he community is doing well.

People always gravitate to areas where there are a lot of jobs. After they get a ob, they need accommodation close by. This is where real estate property ounts. Also, students going to school need a hostel or an apartment close to he university or the college they are going to attend. This will increase the demand for real estate in the community.

hat's why studying and analyzing the economics of the community before nvesting in real estate is very important. Areas where there is the mining of il and natural resources and growth of industries also see a high demand for accommodation. Rural-urban migration is key, and you have to look for small community that is quickly evolving into urban centers.

Look at the vacancy rates, and the average rental cost of the area, th average disposal income of people living there before investing in the propert Simply put, know your market!

The Average Positive Cash Per Property

When you are investing in real estate, you have to be focused on positive cas flow. You've heard this before, "Cash is king!" In real estate, it's not just abou cash, but positive cash flow. Positive cash flow is the amount of money yo made at the end of each month after all expenses have been taken care of. is a critical success factor for investing in real estate property. You don't ca so much as long as you're getting a positive cash flow per month from th property.

The challenge of many real estate traders/flippers is that they get into troub when the real estate market is going down in value. When the market is goin down, they are forced to sell low even though they have bought the underlyin property at a very high price. And this is where positive cash flow real estat investors win the game.

If you're investing for positive cash flow, you will make money in a dow market or an upmarket. This is because even if the market and the economy going down, your property is still in demand and rented by people in th community. You don't make money through the appreciation of the propert but through positive cash flow from the property. This makes the real estat property successful over a long period of time.

Not only do you make money in a down market, but your equity also begins t soar. Positive cash flow means after paying all operating expenses, includin mortgage, you have some money in return. As you service your debt, you equity and net worth will keep going higher. Those positive cash flow from th property can be saved to be used as a down payment to acquire othe properties.

The Financial Analysis of Property

Real estate investing is a plan for financial freedom. Therefore, before buyin a real estate, ask how you how it will impact your current financial conditio Will buying that investment property improves your current financial status c harm it. While you can use external financing opportunities for purchasin properties, you need to understand your current financial status.

After analyzing the financials of the property, consider how it will impact you bottom line. Consider the financial requirements of the property and chec hether you are willing to bear all those risks. Work on the risk analysis of the operty and your financial situation. There are different types of lenders on e market, each having their own terms and conditions. How will another ortgage impact your balance sheet?

re you taking more leverage than you ought to? What is your financial profit, nd how much loan are you permitted to handle? Have you considered hether the rental income of the property will be enough to cover your ortgage, insurance and property taxes? What is the price to rent ratio of the nderlying property you are looking to invest in?

hat is the net operating income (NOI) of the property? How many years will take to cover the costs of the property and pay off the mortgage? You need perform a thorough analysis of the financials regarding the property and en evaluate who it will impact your financial statement and financial status.

The Mortgage Payment

avoid taking yourself into the bankruptcy court, one of the things you have consider before purchasing a real estate property is the mortgage payment. nce real estate properties are very expensive, it's usually very difficult to pay cash upfront for the property. That means using a form of debt to equity tio to finance the property.

ter using a mortgage, you need to calculate and know the exact amount of oney you are required to pay per month. This will help you stay in check and andle the property well to pay for the mortgage. The problem comes when al estate investors are not able to get enough money from the property to ke care of mortgage payments. Normally, this is due to poor financial alysis before taking a mortgage.

check your ability to pay the mortgage required for the property, you need evaluate things like the total monthly income compared to the average onthly debt payment requirements. Standard real estate investment by eddie Mac requires that the average ratio should be 45%. Therefore, alyzing your monthly cash flow and make allowances for times when no one ill rent the apartment and then figure out your ability to fulfill monthly ortgage payment obligations.

The Down Payment for the Property

ost money lenders require at least 25% or 30% minimum down payment for e property and the rest funded through mortgage financing. The rate might very high depending on things like real estate investing experience, credit ore, and cash reserves of the real estate investor.

Down payment for investment properties is normally higher than priva properties. And you need to ensure that you have the cash available to hand both the down payment and the closing costs of the underlying proper Property lenders will not be paying this amount of money for you. This is w you have to analyze the down payment of the property and then figure c how to take care of it.

Successful real estate investors have developed their credibility and th ability to take care of their creditors. They also have a lot of real esta investments under their portfolio, generating enough passive cash flow making down payment and acquiring more properties.

If you're getting started, you might want to have some amount of money your savings account that can be used to take care of your down payment a closing costs for the property. If you've done good homework and have cle credibility, you can leverage all kinds of financing options to raise t remaining capital to purchase the property.

The Rental Yield & Capitalization Rate

If you're going to make money through renting, then you have to carve yc strategy. Are you looking for a short term rental or a long term rental of t property? The Airbnb rental system has become a profit strategy for landlor looking to make money off short term rental of their property. This is inde profitable when you are looking at getting local/foreign tourists in your area rent the property.

Rent is very important in order to generate cash flow to pay for the ren expenses and make the property profitable. If you are considering using t traditional long term rental system, you have to consider the economics of t community and other related factors. The key to getting a high return investment is to make sure you have a regular stream of renters for yc property.

Once you figure out your rental strategy, try to calculate your gross annu rental yield. This is calculated by summing up the annual rent of the prope by the total cost of operating the property and then multiply the figure 100%. The total cost for operating the property will include items such purchase price, closing costs, maintenance cost, and renovations co Knowing your rental yield will enable you to check whether the property is w rented or not.

With your operation cost details, you can even proceed to analyze the c rate/net rental yield of the property. This includes the operating expenses find the net income you would make for renting the property. The total ren income subtracted by the rental expenses will help you know the gross ren ncome made from the property, then you can divide it by the property cost to know your capitalization rate with the final outcome divided by 100%.

CHAPTER SIX: REAL ESTATE MARKETING: HOW TO FIND RENTERS

"Landlords grow rich in their sleep without working."

—John Stuart Mill

Vithout tenants, your real estate will not make any money. The property night be in the right location and have fantastic qualities, but if nobody is enting, you'll not make any money. Just having a property and owning does ot make you a real estate investor. What makes you a real estate investor is our ability to buy, manage, and rent your real estate to generate cash flow.

he game of real estate is a game of cash flow. A real estate is not an asset, s many would say. The property can only be termed as an asset when it puts noney in your pocket, and its value appreciates with time. To be successful in eal estate investing, you need to learn how to get renters to rent your roperty and keep it fully rented.

Jothing brings joy to a real estate investor than to see his/her property full ented by good tenants who are keeping the property well and paying their lue amount of money on time. When this happens, the real estate property ecomes an income-producing machine, running effectively. The investors and reditors are paid, and the deal becomes successful.

But, this is just in theory. While the real estate market is always on an upside, 's not easy to get renters to rent your property, especially when it is not well-ositioned in the right location. For many landlords, getting renters for their roperty takes a lot of blood and sweat. It takes a lot of persistence and letermination to get the right kind of renters for the property.

Three Ways to Get Renters for your Real Estate

t can be very challenging looking for renters for your property. The situation s very hard and difficult when you are in financial distress, and you are ooking for a cash flow system to support you. If you're currently facing that ituation, you don't have to worry about anything. The following are the three deal ways to find renters for your investment real estate properties:

Finding Renters, Yourself

his is the hands-on approach to approach to getting tenants to rent your ouse. With this approach, you have to invest your time, energy, and resources to get tenants and handle the paperwork required to successful rent the property. Even though this process can be time-consuming, it ca also help you to learn how to get to deal with tenants and process tenanc agreements.

The idea here is to promote your vacant units to the point where you g continuous applications. When that happens, you have to screen th application and rent the property to a tenant that will take good care of th place, pay his or her rent on time and make the management of the proper easy and flexible. To promote your site to potential renters in your communit the following are the steps you need to take.

1. Word of Mouth Advertisement

One of the fastest ways you can spread the word about your vacant proper is to simply get the word out through your friends, relatives, coworkers, ar family. When you practice this simple action., you will be excited that a frier will tell a fellow who might be looking to rent the property. By sharing th word and getting the word out, people will begin to realize that you have vacant place for rent available.

If you've taken the time to build your network, you don't have to worry whe you get to this stage. You might have a lot of friends and people who a dealing with real estate. These people can refer tenants to you that will enab you to succeed in your real estate endeavor.

2. Using "For Rent" Sign

This process might not look classy, sexy, and romantic. But, it has been one the oldest and the best ways of marketing real estate for renters. There a many real estate properties that have been rented as a result of using "f rent" signs. Your sign will enable people in the community to know that th property is available for rent. Before you do so, you need to check ar community laws on using these signs. After your post has been accepted, yo can place the "for rent" sign in front of the house, the gate, or closer to th apartment.

3. Using Real Estate Rental Websites

Local for local websites in your community that offers a section f advertisement placement. Contact the real estate website owners and ask you can advertise your website on their sites. These platforms can help yo get the right renters to occupy your rooms.

You should post on various websites and not just one place. If you're lookir for a real estate website to post your rental apartment, some of them incluc Zillow, Tullio. Location is always an important component of real estate. Mak ure you have posted the property at the right location so that you don't get he wring people bidding for the price.

. Social Media Platforms

he incredible power of social media to perform wonders has never been oubted before. Instead of simply providing media for socialization, social edia can help you get tenants for your rental apartment or home. Popular latforms such as Facebook, Twitter, and LinkedIn can be used. If you're using acebook, you might want to post into local Facebook Groups in your area.

/hen you post the picture of the house and the details therein, people within e group living in that area might want to contact you to take a look at the ouse and rent it. Another way of doing this is posting to local groups via /hatsApp or any other platform where the ideal tenants can be found.

. Using Print Media

ow about advertising in your local newspaper, magazine, or trade journal here the ideal customers might see the rental apartments. These mediums ight see to be odd, but you will be surprised at the result you will get when ou publish the stuff in the print media. Contact a journalist or a local ewspaper and then request for a small space to place ads about your partment in the newspaper.

. Using Classified Ad Sites

lassified ads websites might not be your typical real estate website. This latform has been a source of help for many landlords. It's totally free. You ıst have to post to cities where you want to get tenants and then exercise atience for the advertisement to be found. When people start calling you, just ell them about the property and arrange to show them. A good classified ads ite to get started is Craigslist.

here are pros and cons of funding renters by yourself:

The Pros

- You save money: When you look for renters yourself, you save money that will otherwise be paid to real estate agents and real estate management companies to get the job done for you.

- You learn property marketing skills: Since you're doing the job all by yourself, you'll learn skills on how to get renters as you get the job done.

- You do your due diligence to find the right tenants: When you're actively marketing for tenants, you're not looking bad tenants who will damage your property and fail to pay their rents.

This enables you to carefully screen renters before bringing the to your house.

- You are in charge of the renting process: This is ve important because we tend to stay out of control and things g sour or done poorly.

The Cons

- You will need to put in a lot of time, energy and work: Getti renters by yourself might be harder than you will think. Writi your listing, posting into platforms, handling calls and all othe involves a lot of hard work.

- You will need to handle the tenancy application process: t idea of looking for the right tenant can be very hard and difficu You need to understand tenancy contracts and ensure you g your tenants to fill and complete the required tenancy contract f your home.

- Running over on costs: If you don't manage costs very we you might run over and pay much more than you should on your marketing campaigns.

Finding Renters through Real Estate Agents

If you're not the hands-on type of landlord, you can leverage real esta agents to get your home rented faster and quickly. Instead of worryi yourself with all the work that needs to be done to rent your home to go tenants, you simply have to outsource the job to real estate agents who c help. The idea is to rent the property to a real estate agent that deals wi your local area and have a network that can help find renters for your proper

The real estate agent must be experienced, dedicated, and licensed. This w ensure that the job is well done in the right way. Getting a real estate age means that some amount of payment will be made. Real estate agents usua come in two batches, based on what you want. There are some people w will bill the tenants for helping them get a home to rent. However, there a others who will bill the landlord for helping them to get their home.

Choose what you want and look for the real estate agent that will best wo for you. Real estate agents being funded by tenants are working in favor of t tenant. Yet, this does not mean the right thing will not be done. All rental mu be done based on the rental contract and the local tenancy law.

Usually, many real estate agents charge an equivalent of a month's rent f their fee. They only collect their fees when the job is done. So, it's totally risk-free way of getting renters for your home. When you get a real esta agent to help you, they might list your room or home on their advertisement system and help you find a tenant for you using one or more of the following systems:

Local Signs

Most real estate agents have their own signs placed in strategic places that advertise offers they are promoting to the general public. Their signposts can drive a lot of calls in a day that can easily help you get the right tenant for your home.

Agent Website

Many local real estate agents will also publish your rental home on their website. They market and promote your property to a bigger audience to help you get tenants faster. Their website is a well-trusted resource for all tenant-related dealings.

Wider Network

Many real estate agents have their own network of people who already know about what they do. Every day, people keep asking them about homes or apartments to rent. They can be able to link your property to a tenant who might be seriously in need of it.

Multiple Listing Service

All agents within a particular area have an aggregated listing database where their properties can be found. People living in a particular neighborhood can take a look at these properties and contact them to rent. Chances are that your property might be among them and be rented.

Third-Party Rental Websites

Real estate agents and property managers can syndicate property rental ads to many other rental websites to get the right tenants. They simply post one ad on multiple third party websites that will enable them to get who they want. With a simple one-click button, these agents can syndicate to other sites and find the ideal tenant for the property.

Finding Renters through Property Managers

Property Managers here does not refer to a person with a job description as a "property management" professional. These are firms with the expertise of finding tenants for landlords and managing their properties efficiently to generate a profit for them. They, in turn, get paid for their work through the services they deliver to the landlord.

In recent times, the role of property management companies has becom evident, seeing that many owners are looking for ways to scale and grow thei investment properties. Just like real estate agents, they help real estat investors to get the ideal tenants for their homes or properties. But they g the extra mile. They look for the tenant, handle the tenancy contract signin process, lease the property to the tenant, and also manage the tenant so tha everything is successful.

Just like you need to a good real estate agent to enjoy a wealth of knowledg and expertise, a good real estate property management firm will take off you stress of handling and managing a real estate property. They make the wor of taking care of the property easy and stress-free.

Property management firms can be part of a brokerage firm or simply a independent company, working along with real estate investors to ensure tha their properties are 100% rented, well maintained, and managed. Th following entails the ways through which a property management firm ca help in managing and handling the task of getting renters for your real estate.

The fees for property managers take various forms. It varies from one firm t another. The following are some of the pricing/fee models of propert managers: one-time tenant placement, recurring tenant placement one, month off the total rent, and a flat monthly fee. The pricing always varie based on the package and the service structure of the property manager.

If you are looking to leverage the services of property managers to get renter the following are some of the ways you can do that:

Signs

Just like real estate agents, property managers leverage signs in the loca community to find renters for properties they are managing. The exciting thin about signs is that they get results. A good sign placed at strategies places i a particular community will drive a lot of phone calls, which will lead to succes

Property Manager's Websites

Most property managers have a website and have a dedicated column fo placing apartments for rent. Many people visit this website to get informatio and also find apartments to rent. By listing real estate investor's vacant room or apartments on their site, they can be easily able to found by ideal tenants These websites are locally recognized and have high search volume.

Multiple Listing Services

This form of advertisement is also used by real estate managers to hel increase the reach of their client's listing. Since property managers are, t some extent, a licensed real estate broker, they have access to national multiple listing services.

This enables them to list deals of their respective clients on platforms that can easily be recognized. Please, take note that property managers might charge a one month commission on the rental when using this service (If they don't charge a flat monthly fee for their overall service they are providing you).

Syndicated Real Estate Websites

Property managers also leverage independent real estate website to increase the reach of their client's listing. Just like the real estate broker, they syndicate your listing to hundreds of real estate websites in the local area so that you can quickly get your ideal tenant. By levering this scale, property managers are able to fill vacant rooms in short possible time through syndicated real estate websites.

The Pros/Cons of Finding Renters through Real Estate Agents & Property Managers

Real estate agents and property managers function as special assistant to the real estate investor. They help make running a real estate investment property easy. With their help, you can get a lot done in a short period of time. The following entails the pros and cons of real estate agents/property managers:

The Pros (Advantages)

- You get to save time and energy, which can be invested in acquiring new real estate properties.
- You enjoy a wide online coverage and marketing boost, which enables you to get tenants in the shortest possible time.
- You don't have to worry about processing and handling tenant placement and contracts. The real estate agents or property managers take care of this process, based on your arrangement with them, and they take all your stress away.
- You leverage the experience, expertise, and knowledge of real estate agents/property managers to grow your real estate investing business.

The Cons (Disadvantages)

- You will have to pay for professional fees that go along with services being delivered. Unlike real estate agents that may charge a month rent per tenant placement, property managers may even charge monthly management fees or recurring monthl commission.

- You will lose charge or control over some critical areas of you real estate marketing campaign activities.
- You will need to provide certain confidential information to th real estate agent/property managers to enable them to function i their service. This means trusting them and allowing them to ac as custodians of your credentials.

Screening Renters to Weed Out Bad Tenants

The challenge of many real estate investors is renting their apartments to ba tenants who cause a lot of trouble. The way to avoid this problem in the firs place is to screen renters before providing the tenant contract agreement Your listing should be clear as well as pricing to help find the right renters fc the property.

When you get people who want to rent, you need to take their application through a screening process by looking at their details. Check their previou tenant history, criminal history, credit history, employment history, incom profile, and social status to know whether the tenant is a good fit for you property. If you're desperate and fail to look at these critical areas, you'll brin in bad tenants to your house.

Another way to screen is to outline a list of policies in your tenancy contract Your policies might involve taking good care of the property and regularl paying rent. Ensure that the renters comply with the policies before signing it This will ensure you get people who are already in agreement with you. A these things will enable you to get the right tenants to occupy your house an grow your income base.

CHAPTER SEVEN: HOW TO FINANCE & PURCHASE REAL ESTATE PROPERTIES

"Price is what you pay. Value is what you get."

– Warren Buffett

No matter how good a real estate property is, if you don't have the funds to purchase it, you're not going to be a real estate investor. One of the biggest challenges of people looking to go into real estate investing is how they will be able to finance and purchase real estate properties. If you get the financing right, you'll move from the dreaming stage to the action stage, where you're also part of the game.

When you are talking about seeking financing for real estate properties, there are a lot of things to consider. Many of these factors must work together to get the required financing. In fact, many people dread the idea of raising money to buy real estate properties. They think they have no name, brand, or public attention to persuade financiers to invest in their assets.

Well, even you are not a son of Fred Trump, or you have no name in the real estate game, you can still get started. Everyone gets started from the ground up and moves upward. And you see, you don't need millions of dollars to get started. You just have to focus on raising hundreds of dollars to purchase the real estate. As you excel in your business, your asset will begin to grow and your net worth will soar.

More success professionally and financial in the real estate business will convince people to invest in you. Apart from that, you will get to have multiple streams of investment opportunities to use to raise the money you need for your property. All you need is an open mind, persistence and a willingness to push forward to achieve your dreams.

Regardless of where you are now, there's always a way out. Even if the banks are refusing to loan the money to you, there's still an option. You need to have an open mind and always think about how to explore many options to achieve your goal. If you study and learn how to manage the risks associated with real estate investing, you can be on the right side of the game.

3 Key Things to Learn Before Taking Debt

Before you consider exploring opportunities to raise funds for your investment property, you need to develop simple financial habits such as the following:

paying yourself first, improving your credit score and learning how to manag debt. These three cash management skills will help you to raise the mone you need and also help you excel financially.

Paying Yourself First

In George Clason's book, The Richest Man in Babylon, this simple financi principle was first stated. A lot of people know that they have to pa themselves first, but they never do. Successful real estate investors hav developed the habit of paying themselves first. This fundamental financi habit serves as the basis for their big-money deals.

Even before they get started with real estate investing, they developed th habit of saving 10% to 50% of their income and setting it aside f investments. Their consistent saving habit has enabled them to accumulate lot of liquid cash. This is true for real estate investors who run their ov business or work for a company. They know and practice this simple rule.

Paying yourself first enables you to generate cash for investing opportunitie If you learn this habit early on, it can be translated into your real esta investing business. The problem with many real estate investors is that the allow their old money management habits to affect them. They have po spending and saving habit, which cripple their real estate investing.

Some people do save, but they save to spend. The purpose of saving is not buy liabilities and personal effects that lose value over a period of tim Successful real estate investors also save, but they save only to buy asse that generate cash flow and appreciate over a period of time.

Managing Your Credit Score

A credit score is very important in your early days of real estate investing a even years after. If you have a bad credit score, getting private lenders a financial institutions to give you credit will be very hard. Money operates the banner of trust. The more people can trust you, the easier they will gi you credit when you ask them. That's why building and managing your cre score for life is crucial.

Therefore, what you need to do is to analyze your current financial conditi and check how much consumer credit you are bearing. What is your curre score and how are you doing to improve it? If you've developed a b reputation for paying your loans, raising more money will be difficult. This the reason the first principle is crucial.

You need to learn how to budget for surplus instead of a deficit. How do y generate a surplus rather than creating a deficit? Develop ways of reduci your personal expenses and improving your cash flow. Develop a habit frugality and being careful with your personal spending. The key to raising money for real estate always starts with yourself.

If you can't manage your own financial life, how can you manage the cash flow from the property? Consider employing a bookkeeper to start keeping your books and having a professional record of all your business and operational expenses. Keeping track of your cash flow will enable you to correct spending habits and improve your current credit score.

Learning How to Manage Debt

Most people are simply afraid of debt. They try to avoid debt at all cost and they don't want to do anything with debt. Well, if you have this kind of attitude, then you need to drop it. You have to overcome this negative attitude towards debt. If you have this kind of attitude, you'll not be able to raise the amount of money required to finance your real estate properties.

Understand that debt is a form of leverage. And leverage can be used to increase your asset base. The key to managing and improving your debt starts first of all with your financial intelligence. The more financially intelligent you are, the easier it will be to handle and manage debt. As you keep track of your cash flow, keep your books, improve your credit score and pay yourself first, you will increase your financial intelligence and become better at managing debt.

Then, you need to understand that there are two kinds of debt: good debt and bad debt. Bad debt is simply debt that makes you poor, while good debt is debt that makes you rich. Bad debt can be used to acquire assets that generate cash flow and improve your standard of life. When you learn how to acquire, manage and leverage debt to grow your real estate investing business, you'll enter the realm of wealth you never taught of before.

Consider managing and handling debt as good stewardship. A good steward focuses on how to leverage other people's money (OPM) to generate returns that service the debt and still make more money. When you become a good steward of money and have proved faithful in collecting and paying back money to creditors and investors, you'll be successful.

Ways of Raising Money for Real Estate Investing

Once you have developed and leaned the basics, you can proceed with looking for ways to raise money to buy real estate properties. In the beginning, it might be challenging, but as you progress and move on with your real estate investing, you will develop the credibility to raise any amount of money you need for your properties. The following are some of the ways you can use to raise money to purchase investment real estates:

Personal Savings (Cash)

If you have saved up all the money required to buy the underlying property that's really great. You won't have to worry about interest on loans or bearing the risk of real estate foreclosures. Paying all cash for real estate investment property gives you peace of mind and eradicate all kinds of stress-related to raising money to buy real estate.

Also, paying cash for real estate means you have instant equity in the property. Since there is no mortgage payment, the property will instantly be added to your investment portfolio and you can start collecting rent from the property. With additional cash reserved to cater to property maintenance and renovation you can be on your way to enjoying the passive cash flow.

The flipside to using cash to pay for real estate investment properties upfront is having the cash tied up in the property. All your liquid money is locked up in the underlying property and it will take several years to collect the required rent that will cover all the costs of the property. This makes paying in cash not suitable for real estate investors considering renting as a strategy of making money.

But if you want to sell the property and move on to the next thing, then you can get your money out of the property very quickly. This makes paying a cash for property a good deal for real estate flippers. When you buy real estate in an all-cash transaction, you have good negotiation power. You get the best deal and you sell for profit. The profit from your sales can be used to acquire another property.

Whichever way, if you are a real estate investor that is not comfortable with debt financing, you can just pay cash for all your real estate deals. This takes away stress out of the game and you have the required peace you desire. The only thing you might lose is the power of leverage to acquire a lot of properties in a short period of time.

Private Money Lenders

If you have the down payment for the property in cash and the closing costs you can consider using private money lenders to raise the remaining money to buy the property. Private money lenders are simply friends, families, and relatives who have the free cash flow to lend you money to invest in your real estate deals. You already have a good relationship with these investors, which makes things easy when accessing the loans.

When you are dealing with banks and financial institutions, there are lots of regulations and restrictions involved. This is not with private money lenders. This kind of person already knows and trusts you. They believe in you business and want to support you to succeed. As a result, they lend you the money required to finance and purchase the real estate investment property.

When it comes to the length of time to process the loans, it can be a lot faster with private lenders. Once they agree and are okay with the terms, the money can quickly be paid into your bank account for financing. Unlike the regular bank, which might delay the deal just because they want to review the whole deal and property thoroughly to make sure everything is okay, dealing with private lenders can be a lot easier.

Another thing with private lenders is no need to look at a credit score. If you already have investment real estate which makes it difficult for you to lend more money from the traditional banks, turning over to private money lenders is the best thing. It might be very difficult for a traditional bank to understand your condition, but a trusted moneylender will do and give you the money you need.

The cash provided by private money lenders enables you to negotiate a good deal for the property. With cash at hand, your offer will be competitive, and you can get better returns from the property. The usual interest rate of private lenders might range from 7% to 12% with short loan terms. Loans from private money lenders can be used to flip real estate properties or buy and hold to collect rents for a long time.

Before you take loans from private money lenders, you need to ensure that there is a contract in place. If you don't have any contract related to the loan money and things turn sour, it can get really bitter. In fact, the relationship with that friend or family can be destroyed due to financial mishaps. Avoid this problem by ensuring all terms are spelled and a contract has been put in place for the loan amount.

Hard Money Lenders

Hard money lenders are similar to private money lenders. While private money lenders don't have a formalized system of lending money, hard money lenders do. They provide an institutionalized system of raising money to investors. Their funds are also faster and quicker than your traditional loan. In most cases, they will provide you with the loan without considering your credit score. However, financial integrity and trust are crucial.

Hard money lenders provide quick loans based on the value of the property. They analyze the property and know exactly how much money you need to close the deal, and they provide you with the required funding. With experience, trust and knowledge in real estate investing, dealing with hard money, lenders will not be hard at all. You understand the rules of the game and that makes it easy to deal with them.

In recent times, there have been many hard money lenders advertising thei services, and you can contact them to see their offer. The terms of lending ar much more flexible than the traditional bank loan and you can negotiate th terms with the team. This makes hard money lenders a good fit for thos struggling to raise money to buy their real estate properties. Interest rates fo loans might range from 7% to as much as 13%.

But, you also need to understand the flip side of using hard money lenders Since their lending process has been formalized, you'll be required to pay fo things such as loan origination, closing, and closing costs. All this will be pai prior to the processing of the loan. Hard money lenders are referred to a "hard" because they can hijack or come for the property if you default on thei loan and refuse to pay the mortgage payment due to you. Know the terms an conditions before applying.

Fix & Flip Loans

Fix & Flip Loans are not a different class of loans. They are simply a har money loan that is offered to real estate traders who are long for a short terr loan to buy, fix a property and sell it to make their money back. This type c hard money loan is a good fit for all those activities. In some real estat crowdfunding platforms, they also provide room for fix and flip loans. But th terms are usually similar.

While experience and credibility are required to be a successful real estat flipper, you need to understand the market conditions before flipping houses Many people make the mistake of flipping when the market is not doing wel You should know that the game of real estate flipping is to buy low and se high in order to make a profit.

When looking for a hard money loan to fix and flip a house, your person credit score will not be taken into consideration that much. The focus is on th profitability of the real estate. The hard money lender will be lending th money to you because they see value in the property and they believe that th property will sell at a good price and you'll make the ideal profit to pay bac the loan. Analyzing the financials of the property carefully before applying fc the fix and flip loan is very important.

When looking for a fix and flip loan, you need to take into consideration th value of the property after repairs and renovations. Usually, hard mone lenders offer the loan after the look at the estimated value of the propert after the requires have been done. They look at what is known as the AR (after-repair-value) to analyze your ability to pay back the loan.

Again, you have to know the terms and conditions of the loan. The intere rate for fix & flip loans is considerably higher than the usual real estate har noney loans. It ranges around 18% with the time to pay back the principal ınd the interest amount being within a year. Also, you will be required to pay or origination, closing, and loan servicing fees. All this can reduce your ntended profit on the underlying property, but it can be worth the fight!

Traditional Bank Loans

Vhile traditional bank loans are the most attractive form of real estate inancing with a very good interest rate, it can be very hard and challenging to ualify for it. Banks and credit unions are in the business of taking care of ther people's money and they want to make sure that the real estate investor ıas the credentials and the ability to fulfill their loan obligations.

f you meet the demands and requirements of the conventional bank loan, uying real estate properties will become very easy. You will be like Donald rump, able to get huge sums of money from the banks and finance houses to inance real estate properties. But you need to know that the banks and inancial institutions want to deal with experienced real estate investors. xperience counts when you are dealing with traditional bank loans.

lormally, banks and credit unions require that you have at least one-fourth of he property cost yourself, in cash. This normally ranges between 20% to as nuch as 30%) based on the terms and conditions of the loan and other equirements. The riskier the bank considers the real estate investor, the igher the down payment that will be required for the financing of the property.

he following are some of the qualifications or requirements for this type of an: a good credit score, loan affordability based on other monthly obligations, he value & prospectus of the underlying property, the ability of the investor to rove the financials and do the paperwork. In some cases, the banks may equire that you have about six months of mortgage payment in cash before he loan is processed.

ou have to understand that most banks don't consider the future rental from ne property when they are looking at your debt to income ratio. It can get orse before it gets better, but once you learn how to meet the requirements f the banks and credit unions, you can receive unlimited financing to buy as nany real estate properties as possible. Learning to manage all your monthly nortgage payment obligation is crucial.

Joint Venture Financing

ooking for good real estate investment properties is a war on its own. But nen, you are also faced with looking for money for financing. In some cases, ou might not have the full amount of money to cater to the property payment. nstead of worrying about your inability to raise all the money from traditional banks, because you don't qualify, you can simply leverage joint ventur financing.

In this case, what you do is to find a good deal. And then, you contact othe real estate investors who have been in the game for a long time. They migh also be interested in investing in the property in order to reap their interes Many of these joint venture partners have stable businesses and other source of income that pulls in money every money. They have a lot of cash availabl hungrily looking for a place to invest it for better returns.

You can simply present the deal to them and show them how the who property will reap cash flow for all of you. You need to show your joint ventur partners the property cost, the estimated amount of repairs to be done, th estimated rental per month and the property management costs on the re estate. Also, you need to clear about the team of people who will be managin the property. Once your presentation is convincing enough, they can simp pool resources together and help you finance the deal.

You simply have to act as an entrepreneur. You do the work of bringing th deal together while your joint partner finances for the benefit of all of you. some cases, your joint partners will take care of the down payment and th total amount of money required to pay for the property. As usual, you need have a contract and written document for all joint venture finance deals.

Home Equity Financing

Are you looking to move into the home you are considering buying? Maybe is a multi-family home or suite of property and you are considering using part of it and then renting part. You can simply make a down payment on th property, move in and then rent the remaining suite of the property. Luckil the rented portion of the home might even be enough to cater for mortgaged property. This form is known as high ratio financing.

Usually, banks and credit unions consider this safer than engaging in a full re estate investment because they realize you will be living in the property. Yo can use this process to pay for the mortgage on the property and buy mo properties. But, you need to take note of all the real estate laws.

Another way to use home equity financing is to use the value of your home a form of collateral to buy other real estate investment properties. The equi on your existing property will be accessed, and through that, you can apply f a traditional loan to finance the next real estate investment properties. Yo can borrow even up to 80% of the equity of your home for the next deal.

Some home equity financing, such as cash-out refinancing comes with a fixe interest rate, which will be paid during the term of the mortgage. It mig extend the life of the mortgage. Therefore, you need to consider many thin carefully before using it. The most important thing to consider is that you have a place to lay your head. If you fail to take care of the details and requirements regarding the loan, a lot of bad things can happen.

Final Thoughts

Investing in real estate needs to be done carefully and diligently. You need to find a good cash flow property and find the best financing methods for it. While raising money for the property is very important, you need to ensure that all the cash flow management systems are put in place for the success of real estate property.

Contingency plans should be put in place when a lease runs out and tenant is not present to quickly take care of the mortgage on the property. Examine your financing conditions carefully before taking any form of a loan. Also, ensure that all real estate loans are taken through a limited liability company to avoid any personal damages when things don’t go your way.

CHAPTER EIGHT: BASIC ACCOUNTING FOR REAL ESTATE INVESTORS

"Never take your eyes off the cash flow because it's the lifeblood of business."
—Sir Richard Branson

One of the most challenging and tedious parts of running a real estate investment is keeping the books. Many real estate investors don't keep their books. They prefer to figure things out in their heads rather than prepare professional records for their business. They fail to keep their books; therefore, they fail to manage their real estate investments very well.

Accounting for a real estate is not different from that of a business. The operations are different, yet the same principles and concepts apply. Just as you need to have a balance sheet, income & loss statement and a cash flow statement for a business, you need to have the same thing for a real estate. The key to success in real estate investing is to think of your operation as a business and see yourself as an entrepreneur.

Once you begin to think in this way, you need to understand the concept of separation in accounting. You are a separate entity from the business. That means there must be a separate accounting from the real estate, exclusive of you. There must be a clear financial statement for the real estate that shows its profitability. Instead of juggling the real estate funds with your own personal cash, you have to separate them.

When you perceive and see yourself as a shareholder of the company, you will tend to have a better view of the business. You will have a separate professional statement of accounts for the business and then review the reports regularly for effective management. When you begin to run your real estate from the numbers instead of the assumption, you'll be experience profit and growth.

Why Accounting for Real Estate?

If you're not still convinced about the importance of bookkeeping and accounting for real estate, the following should help you chart the course:

Real Estate Accounting Helps to Control the Cash Flow of the Property

Management guru, Peter Drucker said, "If you can't measure it, then you can't manage it." How then do you expect to manage your cash flow well if you don't keep track of it? In fact, it is just impossible to keep track of your cash flow if you don't keep the books. By checking and looking into the books, you can be well-positioned to make the right decisions that will make the property do well.

Identify Performing and Non-Performing Real Estate Properties

If you're going to do well in all the properties you are running, then reports need to be created for them. Each house that you have a business and must have a financial report. Businesses established a branch and then have a branch manager ensure that financial records are kept for the business. To do well, you need to ensure each of your homes has its own financial recording. This will enable us to monitor and know which performing well and which does not need it.

Compare Year-To-Year Financial Growth of the Property

As a real estate investor, your financial records is your scorecard. You can measure and analyze the growth of your real estate business by comparing the financial performance of one year against the other. Doing this helps you to know whether you're beating the past records of you're just clinging to the status quo. The year-to-year reports help to adopt new strategies and policies to grow the business.

Provide the Financial Report to Raise Capital

If you're going to raise money from investors, they need to know your current financial position. The only way to show it is through financial reports. Without good financial reports of your real estate business, getting a loan from investors and the banks will be very hard.

By keeping good financial reports for your real estate business, investors will realize you're serious about your business and will be more than willing to invest if your records show that the property is growing, and you need financial assistance to get to the next level.

Real Estate Performance Measurement Metrics

Lenders require you to provide your profit & loss/income statement and the Balance Sheet/Statement of Financial Position.

- ***The Income Statement*:** It shows all rental income and expenses (operating expenses and fixed expenses) for a period (it could be monthly, quarterly or annually) The income statement tells how profitable your real estate investment is.

- ***The Balance Sheet*:** It provides a list of assets, liabilities, and equity of the owner. The asset, in this case, might be your house. The liabilities will have to include the mortgage. The retained earnings of property, as well as the initial down payment of the owner, will entail the owner's equity. The assets must be equal to the liabilities for the account to balance.

- ***Cash Flow Statement*:** This helps you to know your current financial position and, therefore the cash movement in the real estate. The cash flow statement should provide your net operating, financing and investing cash flow.

Apart from this, there are other financial ratios critical for managing a real estate. They include the following: gross rent multiplier (GRM), net operating income (NOI), the capitalization rate and cash on cash return.

- ***Net Operating Income (NOI)*:** It refers to the total gross scheduled rent minus all expenses and maintenance estimates. The property expenses might include things like insurance premiums, taxes, property management fee and many others. It can be found as follows: *"NOI = Gross Scheduled Rent - Operating Expenses - Maintenance and Vacancy Estimates."*

- ***Gross Rent Multiplier (GDM):*** It used to help you know how many years the rental from the property can be bel to pay for the property cost. The lower the property cost, the better. Ideally, the calculations can be found as follow: *"GRM = Purchase Price / Annual Gross Scheduled Rent."*

- ***Cap Rate:*** It takes into account the net operating income by the purchase price. This is an important metric for buying and analyzing how profitable a real estate property. The calculation for the cap rate can be calculated as follows: "Cap Rate = Annual NOI / Purchase Price."

- ***Cash on Cash Return*:** After using leverage to acquire a property, you want to know how profitable the whole deal looks like. The cash-on-cash return helps to calculate the return on the total cash invested while taking into account the leverage expense of the property. It can be calculated as follows: "Cash on Cash Return = Net Annual Cash Flow / Total Cash Invested."

Real Estate Accounting Tips

Again, it is very important that you get a bookkeeper to keep your books Trying to save money on bookkeeping instead of hiring the services of a accountant or outsourcing to an accounting firm will not enable you to gro your real estate portfolio.

To build a real estate empire, it is very important that you invest the require amount of money to get your books kept in a professional manner.

1. *Assume that your real estate property is a business*. In th case, you bought a business that is your property, and it needs t have an income statement that shows its profitability and balance sheet that shows its financial position.

2. *Have all operations of the property recorded professionally* With the help of your bookkeeper, you can start keeping track your fixed and operating expenses. You should take into accou the payment of taxes and monthly mortgage payments. All rent income should be recorded as an expense.

3. *Prepare monthly, quarterly and annual reports of yo financial position*: To ensure you do well financially, provic regular reports for your real estate investments. These repor should be used to enhance the effective management of th property.

4. *Have a periodic financial review with your account/bookkeep* At the end of each month, quarter or year, ensure you do review of your financial reports with your team. This will help track financial problems before they happen.

In keeping your books, you might also want to leverage digital tools to ma the job easier. Cloud accounting software has been tremendously helpful. Th following are some of the accounting software that will be helpful for your re estate investing: Wave, QuickBooks, Sage, FreshBooks, Zoho, and ma others. You also need a photocopier machine and scanner to help provi other documents essential for your financial reports.

CHAPTER NINE: HOW TO REPAIR, MAINTAIN & MANAGE REAL ESTATE PROPERTIES

"Real estate practice is not about selling or buying a home. It's about representing your client's greatest asset to your client's greatest benefit."

– Alex Delgado

As a real estate investor, the importance of repairing, maintaining, and managing a real estate property cannot be underestimated. Successful real estate investors are known for keeping well managed, removed and clean investment properties that become an envy of the market. Their meticulous attention and dedication towards maintenance are some of the things that give them a tremendous competitive advantage in the market.

If you are looking to become a successful real estate investor, then you need to take property management as a very important part of the game. If you take good care of the property, it will take good care of the tenants, which who eventually will take good care of you financially. Not only will your property be fully rented by the right tenants, but it will also increase in value over time.

This is a secret many mediocre real estate investor fails to learn. They think real estate investing is just about buying and selling properties. It goes beyond that. Property management is what serves the difference between one real estate property and another. This is the reason Alex Delgado said, *"Real estate practice is not about selling or buying a home. It's about representing your client's greatest asset to your client's greatest benefit."*

What you want to do is to make the property of great value to the client that he/she cannot but to pay the required amount to rent the property. In fact, you can even increase rents when renovations on the underlying property contribute to a high standard of living for tenants. That means more cash flow from the property. When it comes to property management, all it takes is a little creativity and innovation, and you can make your tenants happy.

Usually, tenants are happy and proud of their residence when it is highly maintained. They bring their relatives, friends, acquaintance, and business associates to the place because of superb it is. This provides you with free publicity. Usually, most tenants are more than willing to pay a top dollar when they realized that the tenant is taking good care of the property and making them feel better. This is why you can't take property management for granted if you want to be very successful in real estate investing.

Why Property Maintenance?

Property maintenance involves the all-encompassing activity of inspecting, repairing, replacing and renovating a real estate property to ensure that it is kept in good condition, free any kind of damage that might destroy it. Maintaining a real estate is a full-time job that should be done well if you are looking to get the maximum result. The problem with many landlords is that they wait until issues begin to compound before they start dealing with them.

Good property management ensures that you anticipate or inspect the underlying property regularly so that you can resolve issues before they emerge or exacerbate. These days, many tenants have become very keen on the landlord-tenant law, which underlines when and how often a property is supposed to be maintained in order to meet the rental requirement and to be considered safe for the public.

If you don't know how to get a handle of the property maintenance thing, you can simply refer to your local landlord-tenant law and look at what it says about managing and maintaining a real estate property. This will ensure that you maintain the property properly and keep it a good condition for tenants. Always remember that a good property makes happy tenants.

Apart from reading the landlord-tenant law to know how to deal with property management, you can conduct research to learn simple and creative ways to add value to your real estate investment property. Landscaping projects such as creating a garden, a yard, pathway, outdoor section, and painting are all fascinating. Sometimes, only a little renovation is all it takes to give a new facelift to old real estate property. Hence, property management is essential for real estate investing success.

Key Things to Know About Property Maintenance

The goal of many real estate investors is to buy a property and bring it to the marketplace and collect rents. While this might seem exciting, many landlords seem to forget and figure out the need for regular property maintenance. Well, the following are some key things about property maintenance you have to keep at the back of your mind when you are considering buying and investing in real estate:

Always Maintain a Standard Building Code

Yes, you want to start collecting rent. But, your tenant wants to ensure that they will enjoy the best possible life when they rent your property. This is why you need to ensure that you maintain a standard building code for all your real estate investment properties. You need to ensure that your properties are fit to a certain level and standard before putting them into the market for rent or sale.

If you fail to deal with critical housing systems such as electricals, plumbing, sewerage, waste management, heating & cooling, a supply of electrical energy, electrical wiring, the flow of water, safety of electrical appliance and many others, you'll face a lot of problem with tenants. Tenants don't want to come home and find their possessions on fire because of poor electrical wiring in the house or having no water to shower. Maintain a standard code before putting a property for rent.

Always Factor Unexpected Property Maintenance as Part of the Operating Expense of the Property

It is very important to always budget for property maintenance before it is even needed. Taking good care of your property in real estate investing is not an option; it is a necessity. Many beginner real estate investors are just hoping and praying that their property never has any expenses. While that's good, property maintenance will always come from time to time, and you need to plan towards it.

Not planning for regular and continuous property maintenance is a recipe for disaster. Ideally, consider setting aside at least 10% of monthly rental income towards property maintenance. That does not mean you should blow the money when the property does not really need any maintenance at the moment. But, the essence of it is to ensure that you're proactive with your property maintenance. Budgeting for unexpected and regular expenses keeps you on top of the property maintenance demands of the asset.

Always Be Prompt and Quick in Dealing with Emergency Property Maintenance

Shockingly, some real estate investors seem not to care about emergency maintenance on their property. After they have rented the property, they go to sleep and wake up ready to collect their rents/renewal lease payments. You need to understand that you're in business and your tenants are your clients.

Failing to promptly deal with emergency property issue exposes the life of the tenants to danger, and you're the one responsible. A breakdown of the housing leading to severe injuries of tenants can cost you a lawsuit and drain your real estate investment capital. This is why it's very important that you are always prompt in dealing with any emergency repair or replacement that a tenant informs you about. This even saves you a lot of dangers when you take care of them quickly. The tenants are in your hands, and you have a responsibility to keep them safe, secure and sound.

Always Take Care of Turnover Repairs Before Placing the Apartment for Rent

Tenants are required to bear any cost of the damage they have incurred to the property during their stay. Before departing or vacating the rental unit, they are required to ensure that the property has been cleaned and tidied. However normal wear and tear of the house will require that certain renovations be done before renting the apartment to the next tenant. This is where your responsibility as the landlord comes!

It should start by inspecting the property to look at areas that need some form of work. Consider planning for normal turnover expenses such as painting landscaping, changing locks and carpet cleaning of the apartment. Taking care of all these repairs before putting the property for sale will ensure that you get high-quality renters who will be willing to rent the property.

Maintaining Regular Property Inspections

As a rule of thumb, always schedule a regular inspection code of the property Inspection is crucial if you want to spot problems before they emerge. You can wait for plumbing problems to start developing before you solve them, or you can schedule regular inspections of your plumbing system to ensure all leaking pipes are handled.

Another typical area that requires regular inspection is roofing. Sometimes you might not notice that you have a roofing problem until there is rainfall Leaving leaks in the plumbing system of your toilet undone can cause serious problems for tenants in the house. All these things require regular property inspections to avoid having big problems.

Bringing building experts from time-to-time to check on your property is very important. By scheduling a regular inspection, you can catch these small problems and repair them quickly. Failing to do regular plumbing, roofing drainage, electrical and other forms of inspections can lead to serious damage to your house before you know.

Four Types of Property Inspections

To get started with your property inspections, you need to know and understand the various kinds of inspection undertake on your property. Just jumping with regular inspection might be good, but not very effective in enhancing a 100% maintenance of your property. So, the following are various property inspection types you need to be aware of:

1. Move-Out Property inspection

This kind of inspection is very important as it will prepare the rental property for the next tenant. It helps to know the kind of maintenance required to ensure the property is clean, organized and ready for the next tenant who will be renting it. You get to know the kind of wear and tears that must be done on the property. There are some cases when the current tent needs to be responsible for some repairs due to damages that might have been caused to the property. This kind of inspection help you to figure this out before the tenant vacates the premises.

2. Routine Property Inspection

If you want to ensure that your real estate property is always fit, then routine maintenance is a must. You can range quarterly routine maintenance of the entire property so that you can handle all kinds of issues before they degenerate. Communicating with tenants and discussing with them about possible damages and repairs that needed to be done is a great way to save a lot of hard work.

3. Move-In Property Inspection

This kind of inspection is very important because it helps the landlord and the tenant to know the state of the property before it was rented. All conditions of the property will be inspected and detailed in the rental lease that will be signed. The landlord expects that the property should be kept in good condition and there should be no damages except occasional repairs during turnover.

4. Drive-By Property Inspection

To make sure that your property is in good condition, you can routinely or occasionally check the interior and exterior unit of the house to see if everything is in order. You might be able to notice little cracks and leaks that should be handled immediately.

Interior & Exterior Unit Inspection

While there are four types of inspection to be carried about on your real estate investment property, there are two main units that must be inspected. Real estate problems either come from the exterior or the exterior units of the property. When inspecting a property, you want to ensure that all these areas are well checked and issued noted for immediate repairs.

Just like Richard Branson, taking notes of issues he sees in his Virgin Airways, consider your real estate investment as a business. Inspect and take notes of problems you think they need to be taken care of and solved well. When you spot a problem with ant part of the property, or a tenant has informed you take a look at it and record it in your notebook for repairs.

The following are the critical exterior and interior units of the underlying property that needs to be invested each time a real estate inspection exercise is being performed:

Interior Unit Inspection

- Heating & cooling system: Ensure that the filters of the heating and cooling system have been checked regularly to ensure that they are not dirty or inhibited by any foreign material or mold. If the air filter is blocked by any foreign material, it will prevent the free flow of fresh/cool air.

- Interior Painting: You want to ensure that there is no mold growing on the walls and causing the paints to be chipping off the wall. Regularly have the tenants report any incidence of that sort and there get the appropriate experts to repair the interior to ensure everything looks beautiful.

- Smoke detectors: You don't want to live in a room without a smoke detector, do you? No. Neither do your tenants want to live in an apartment where the is no smoke detector? This can be very dangerous and can lead to many unprecedented accidents in the home when an electrical explosion from somewhere emerges.

- Water heater: Checking water heater regularly to ensure that they function well is key to a good interior property inspection Most people are very attentive to their water heater and that doesn't want to be seeing any dirt from the water because there are all sediments in the water. Focusing on working to improve property management systems.

Exterior Unit Inspection

- Exterior Painting: Most tenants hates and abhors houses that look dirty and terrible on the outside. They don't feel happy and comfortable. Refusal to paint the exterior of your house when you have to says a lot about you as the tenant. You want to ensure your property reflects your values of neatness and beauty. Ensuring that the exterior of your house is well painted helps to prevent it from damages from the sun and moisture.

- The roof: Living in a leaking roof is like living in hell. When it rains, you can't help yourself. If your house has roofing problems you might want to deal with it and ensure that everything is in good condition before renting. Mold growth, damages, and leaks need to be dealt with for tenants to be safe at night.

- Windows: It's amazing that some rooms don't have windows or they have a poor ventilation system. This tends to drive many tenants away from renting the property. You also want to make sure that the windows of the property are well sealed to avoid during the time of heating and insulation. Old and window repairs need to be taken care of.

- Landscape: A good landscape adds to the aesthetic, beauty and color of the home. You want to ensure that all trees are well trimmed, and those needing cutting are done well. All gardens must be taken care of and grasses kept green. A well-maintained landscape speaks volumes about the house and the landlord.

Do it Yourself (DIY) & Done for You (DFY) Property Maintenance

Property maintenance is key for a successful real estate investment. Poorly managed and maintained real estate will obviously fail, no matter all the benefits of real estate investors. Therefore, you need to take your property maintenance seriously if you're going to do well. You need to analyze and decide on which approach you want to use to manage the underlying property.

Generally, there are two main options:

Do it Yourself (DIY) Property Maintenance

As the landlord, you have the responsibility for your house. You can choose to manage all kinds of inspection, repair, and maintenance related to your property. Ideally, this will save your money each month and year. To get the job done, you must leverage the service of other contractors like plumbers, electricians, roofing contractors, painters, and building contractors.

You also need to oversee the work that is done by these professionals to ensure that you get value for your money. Handling all kinds of inspection and maintenance works related to your property takes a lot of time and attention, which can be spent on other real estate investing activities. In addition, you need to make sure you have the right skill set and experience to handle the property management tasks. If you're finding the task challenging, you might want a second option.

Done for Your (DFY) Property Maintenance

Property Management companies have the skill, experience, and time to take care of your property. They know how to keep your property well maintained and renovated so that it is sparkling. Many of these firms have years of experience in the field and their expertise in the field is really breathtaking. When you outsource your maintenance to a credible property management company, you can lessen the burden of running a real estate property.

They will save you time and money in the long term and increase the value of your property over time. For real estate investor who doesn't want to be called at night about fixing toilets and dealing with plumbing work, you can simply outsource the job to a very good property management company who can get the job done. From the exterior to the interior section, the property manager will schedule routine inspections with regular maintenance to keep the property in good condition for you.

You might, however, be required to pay monthly property management fees. There is some property management company who even take care of the tenants in the property as well as the property. That means you can scale your real estate investing business. You just have the property management company help rent tenants for you, lease the property, manage the tenant and keep the property in good condition. The challenge is finding an outstanding property manager with a good track record.

It can be tempting for new real estate investors to want to save money and do the job all by themselves. But the issue is that you can grow a real estate investment empire if you want to be doing all kinds of work related to the property. Leveraging the services of property managers is very important if you want to reduce the workload on you and focus on other things.

Property Maintenance Tips

Andrew Syrios, a successful real estate investor, said concerning property maintenance: "Maintenance is the face of your company, and good maintenance is the best form of tenant retention there is. Many tenants are used to poor quality service, so if they come to your place and get good service, it substantially increases the chance that they will want to continue renting from you."

To ensure your tenants are happy, good property maintenance is not optional. The following property maintenance tips will help you as you work on developing and improving your real estate investment property.

1. Be on the lookout for all kinds leaks, from roofing to plumbing after a severe storm, flooding and water damage. Arrange with experts to fix these things.

2. Ensure that you have fire extinguishers in the house and they are working well.

3. Regularly fix the heating and cooling systems and replace air filters.

4. All gutters and drainage systems in the house should be clean and tidy.

5. The house should always be clean and neat at all times.

6. Set up a system that ensures that tenants clean the house and keep the property in good shape.

7. All smoke detectors in the house should be check regularly and fixed.

8. Arrange with a gardener to keep all trees, yards, and flowers in good shape.

9. Ensure that mold and leaks do not develop in the showering system.

10. Pests and insects should be constantly be inspected and exterminated from the house.

11. Water heaters should be flushed regularly.

12. All toilets and bathrooms in the house should be kept clean.

13. Sewerage and waste management system should be handled well.

14. Constantly check locks and safes in the house to ensure they are in good shape.

15. Fence the house to avoid thieves breaking into the house. If possible, set up a security system.

Regular property maintenance will not only keep your property in good shape, but it reduces your costs of running the property. It will save you money. Therefore, consider who will take care of the property and get the job done well. As the landlord and the real estate investor, do you have the skills and expertise to provide efficient management for the property? Can you get the job done well? If you can't, simply look for a good property manager and negotiate a good price. Then outsource the management so that you can focus on growing your real estate investment business.

CHAPTER TEN: HOW TO BUILD YOUR OWN REAL ESTATE INVESTMENT EMPIRE

"Buying real estate is not only the best way, the quickest way, the safest way,

but the only way to become wealthy."

– Marshall Field

If you have a goal of building a real estate investment empire, you'll have to keep in mind that it is possible. Many of the super successful real estate investors you see today have all started from the same spot as you. Nobody starts from the top, everyone starts from the bottom and then climbs to the top. That should be your objective more than anything else.

Building a real estate investment empire will take you years of studying, learning, and practicing. Through the years, you'll learn all the basic skills of real estate investment. You will get to learn how to purchase, managed and rent real estate property to collect rent or even sell the property to realize a profit from the transaction.

While you need to think big, you'll have to think small. The secret of success in real estate is not in the big things you do. Rather, the secrets of your success can be found in your daily goals, agendas, and routines. The way you spend your time and money is a reflection of your focus towards achieving your goal of building a real estate empire.

Action Steps to Building Your Own Real Estate Empire

To pursue your goal of building a real estate empire, there are certain steps you must commit yourself to in order to get there. The following are just but a few of them. These simple steps can help take your dream into reality and enable you to build the real estate investment empire you desire:

Studying and Learning from the Experts

If you have a goal of building a real estate investing business, then the first place to get started is to have some heroes in the field that you admire. Once you've got your real estate investing heroes, the next step is to start learning from them. You need to learn as much you can about how they got started when they got started, the challenges they faced along the way, and how they were able to overcome them.

Having a good grasp of this information will prepare you mentally and emotionally to get started with real estate investing. Seeing from the eyes of experts will help to purify your thoughts and assumptions that you might have personally developed with regard to real estate investing. Chances are that some of them might already have written books, created podcasts and videos with regarding their areas of expertise.

You have to get all this information. It's crucial. You want to learn how they made and also gain insights on how to get yours done. Some of the most successful and famous real estate investors you can consider learning from are Sheldon Anderson, Robert T. Kiyosaki, Grant Cardon, Donald Trump, and many others.

Developing Your Real Estate Investing Plan

Consider real estate investing as a business. Just like any business, you don't want to get started with no plan in place on what to do and how to do it. You need a plan to get started in real estate investing. If you're going to be flying an airplane, you can just enter and start moving. You need a clear, concise and realistic plan to move the plane to the right destination.

Your real estate plan should start with your niche. Which area of real estate do you want to trade? What skills and expertise do you need to learn to get started? What are your pain points with regards to your real estate investing plan? Which people do you want to consider bringing on your board? Have you thought about financing? How do you intend to raise funds to grow your business? What's your plan to ensure that the property is well maintained and managed?

How many real estate portfolio are you looking to have in your portfolio? You need to understand the rudiments and parameters you will be using to run your real estate. Have you done your financials? How much money is estimated to gets started with real estate investing? Do you have a plan in place to raise funds needed to start with your first investment real estate?

Part of the plan also entails developing the right mindset and traits of highly successful real estate investors. You need to learn to think right if you're going to be successful in real estate investing. You must develop the plan to build your network and cultivate the necessary relationships for success.

Building Enough Personal Equity Capital

What really stops many people from starting their own real estate investment business is the fact of not getting money to buy properties. They are concerned about the money they need for their own personal survival, and therefore they fail to build enough savings to serve as a cushion for their real esta business. Before you start investing in real estate, you have to be reminded that you'll need to have an income stream that already feeds you.

Consider developing the habit of savings with your current business or job. Create a separate bank account where you can save money regularly towards your real estate investment business. Set a goal of saving about $ 50,000, $ 100,000, and even much more than that in cash. Set aside cash to support you as you learn and study to become a successful real estate investor.

The savings are not for any kind of spending. They will be used as a down payment for your first investment real estate property. What you want to do is to make sure you have cash available to make the down payment of your first property and then use other means to raise the necessary cash to purchase the real estate investment property. Having your first down payment in cash will save you a lot of headaches that come with buying real estate properties.

Register a Limited Liability Company and Separate Business Bank Account

It is very important that you don't buy real estate properties in your name. You need to ensure that you register a liability company that will represent the company. You should be doing all real estate investment operations through this company. Consider your limited liability as a real estate investment holding company. The entity you are registering will handle all your operations.

Registering a limited liability company requires a lot of regulations. Consider if you have the skills and the education required to register the company or you can consider talking to an attorney to help you with all the documents are fillings you need to get the real estate investment company registered. Ensure that all details for the company are right and accurate.

You will be asked to get a company secretary and director. Consider talking to a trusted associate to fill in this position for you. If you have a partner who you want to run the business, that fellow can be your director. Prepare all documents, fill the required forms and finally have the real estate investment registered as a limited liability company.

You will be asked to create a Tax ID for the company. This will be served as your employment tax ID. All taxes related to the real estate investment company will be processed through this ID. If you happen to get employees or staff for your company in the future, all tax withholdings will be processed via this place.

Once the company has been registered, the document should be used to open a separate bank account for the company. All business-related transactions should be dealt with through this particular account. The fact is that you don't want to be paying for real estate properties through your personal bank account. Once you open the bank account, deposit the savings you made into the real estate investment bank account.

Start Investing In Real Estate

You can never become a successful real estate investor if you don't take the first step. This is where most people really miss it. They talk too much, but they never take action. They dream a lot, yet their dreams never come to reality because they lack the discipline to work on their dream and make it real. If you're going to be successful in real estate investment you must be action-oriented.

Just talking about your dream of building a real estate empire will get you nowhere. Therefore, the sooner you get started with your dream, the faster you will get there. That means setting a goal, making plans, and taking action required to purchase your first investment real estate. If you've been building your savings regularly, creating a business account, and creating a corporate entity for the real estate, you might have even laid the foundation to start.

You have to start small. Start with small real estate investment properties and then grow from there to bigger projects. Look for projects that you can make a cash down payment and then use leverage to pay the remaining down payment. The first few real estate properties you will start will build your confidence to go onto bigger deals. They will also enable you to gain real-life experience in real estate and develop your real estate investing skills.

As you start with your real estate investment, you might want to create a digital presence. You can consider creating a website for your real estate investing business. And then create your own self hosted email. While you can use the generic Gmail or Yahoo mail for business, it will not make you look professional for people who might want to invest or do business with you in the future.

The best you have to do is create a business website and a business email on the domain name. For example, you could have a website like www.ExploreRealEstates.com, and then you have an email like info@explorerealestates.com. Having the right digital presence for your real estate business creates an impression of success and professionalism from the beginning. You might start a podcast or a blog series about your experience in real estate. All this builds a resource and tells potential investors that you are serious about what you are doing.

Building your Real Estate Investing Team

If you want to scale your real estate investment business, you can't do it all alone. You have to think about involving a team. You have so many hours a day. If you're going to build a real estate investment empire, you really can't do it all by yourself. This is where leadership, cooperation, and team building comes. Many people tend to be weak in leadership and team building. As a result, they aren't able to build the real estate investment business they desire.

In his book, the *17 Indisputable Laws of Teamwork*, John Maxwell said, "As much as we admire solo achievement, the truth is that no lone individual has done anything of value. The belief that one person can do something great is a myth. There are no real Rambo' who can take a hostile army by themselves. Even the Lone Ranger wasn't really a loner. Everywhere he went, he rose with Tonto! Nothing of significance was ever achieved by an individual acting alone."

It takes a team to make a dream work. To take it further, it takes a great team to make a great dream work. The quality of your team will determine the height of your accomplishment. The weaker your team, the lower the morale and the productivity will be. Therefore, you need to focus on assembling the right team to handle the various operation of the real estate investment. All these teams must be unified by a common goal, aim, objective, or mission.

When your entire team is on the same page, you will accelerate and achieve bigger things with time. What are the people needed to scale your one-man army real estate business? Which people do you need, and what values must they hold? Be clear about your own vision, mission, and values and then use them as a yardstick to enlist the services of people you need. At a minimum, you need a banker, bookkeeper/accountant, attorney, real estate broker, property manager, and many others as the number of your real estate holdings grow.

Reinvesting and Building Your Portfolio

As you make profits, you have to learn to reinvest those profits back into the business. When you sell a real estate property, use the funds to buy a bigger one instead of spending it on your personal stuff. Reinvesting your profits and managing your cash flow very well is key if you're going to be successful in building your portfolio.

Relying on your rental income for living expenses will not help you to build your real estate investment empire. Rental income from the property must be saved and used as a down payment for the next real estate property. This is why it is very important to develop a strong habit of disciplined spending, frugality and saving early on before you start your real estate business.

By reinvesting profits, rather than spending it, you will build trust from your investors and bankers. You will also build strong cash reserves that will qualify you for traditional loans with better interest rates, which will grow your portfolio easily. While leverage is good for real estate, you want a good offer. And it comes when you learn to reinvest profits back and manage your cash flow effectively.

CHAPTER ELEVEN: REAL ESTATE INVESTING MISTAKES TO AVOID

"To be successful in real estate, you must always and consistently put your clients' best interests first. When you do, your personal needs will be realized beyond your greatest expectations."

– Anthony Hitt

Today, there are countless blogs, podcasts, YouTube, and TV Programs with many so-called "multimillion real estate investors" who preach that real estate investing is easy and the safest way to create great wealth. Well, while many wealthy people have used real estate investing as a vehicle to build their financial empire, it is important to know that success in real estate doesn't come by chance.

It requires a lot of sacrifices, hard work, focus and perseverance to succeed. If you're not committed to the game, you're not going to make it. Real estate investing involves dealing with a lot of money, and if you lose focus, you can just sink the financial ship and have a shipwreck. This is why staying objective when it comes to real estate is crucial.

Unfortunately, the problem with many beginner investors is that they think it is so easy. They make a mistake of thinking real estate investing is very cheap and easy, which makes them not to give the required attention needed for success. This is one of the things that have crippled many real estate investors. They assume that everything will be cool and when they face reality, they run into debt and declare bankruptcy.

"The reality is, real estate investing isn't always as rosy or predictable as the TV shows make it out to be. This is true whether you invest in homes to 'flip' them for new buyers, or whether you invest in rental properties to build long-term, passive income," says Holly Johnson.

Mistakes to Avoid in Real Estate Investing

Real estate investing is not like investing in stocks, bonds, ETFs and mutual funds. These investment vehicles require less attention and control. After you have invested your money, you don't have to actively manage the investment in order to generate a return. For example, when you invest in a dividend-paying stock, you receive monthly and quarterly payments without doing any work.

This is different when it comes to real estate investing. You have to understand the market and ensure that all the properties are well managed to be profitable in the long term. That's the reason Terrel Gates, a successful real estate investor and portfolio manager, said, "Unfortunately, to be consistently successful in real estate over the long haul requires more skill than luck."

The following are some of the notable mistakes you have to avoid while investing in real estate.

Not Doing a Professional Inspection Before Buying

So, you want to save money on a professional inspection. As a result, you did not do good research or professional inspection before buying the property. As a result, you ended up spending a lot of money on renovation and maintenance than you should. This simply leads to high operating costs, which tend to create a lot of problems.

Hiring a professional real estate inspector will help you analyze the status of the property and the estimated amount of money you will spend to renovate before renting or selling it. Getting a professional home inspector will reveal any hidden costs that you might not see at first. It will also help you avoid buying real estate properties that will become a liability rather than an asset.

Avoid buying real estate properties without doing a professional inspection. Before you make any purchase, check whether the property is worth the price, investing, and managing to generate the estimated returns. If you notice that the property is will not help you, just cut your losses and move onto the next property.

Not Keeping an Eye on the Numbers

If you're not good with accounting, real estate investing can be big trouble for you. When you are using other people's money to invest in real estate, you are accountable. You need to ensure that all funds invested in the property are well managed. And that means keeping regular attention on the numbers of the game.

If you don't keep your books or your books are not well kept, you're not going to make it. You might run into serious losses as a result of poor financial record keeping. To be a professional real estate investor that banks, credit unions, and other investors will trust, you need to maintain clean financial records of your business.

And you must have your financial team produce weekly, monthly, quarterly and annual financial reports that will help you keep the focus on building the business. Have a clear idea of your mortgage, tax, operating costs, prof margin, and all others before buying a property. As rich dad said, "Your profit is made when you buy, not when you sell."

Not Building Enough Cash Reserves

In real estate investing, cash is king. After you purchase the real estate, you need cash to maintain and manage the property. If you don't have the required cash to get the whole business going, you can be in trouble. For example, you want to make sure you have can set aside for unexpected vacancies before they happen.

This can help you take care of your mortgage and tax payments so that you don't have any problem. You might also decide to plan for unexpected repairs and renovations, which might happen in the process of time. Building a strong cash reserve will help you to weather both bull and bull market. When the market is tough, your cash reserves can keep you going before everything turns out well.

Seasoned real estate investors are known to set aside about 10% to 20% of their annual rental income as a reserve to take care of anything that might happen. This cash serves a cushion to prevent shocks that can damage your real estate empire.

Not Screening Tenants Before Renting

In haste to start collecting rents, many real estate investors just go for a bunch of low-quality tenants that give them a lot of headaches. The tenant avoids paying rents, mismanage, and damage the property. They quarrel with their tenants and landlord and make a living in the house unbearable. This kind of tenants must be screened and avoid in the first place.

Just because a person has money to rent does not mean you should rent for them. You've got to set a standard and detail the type of tenant you want. When you run your add, you should make it known to those who show up about your terms and conditions.

Check the credit and criminal history of the tenants before renting your property to them. While you need to screen tenants, you must also avoid any act of discrimination in relation to sex, religion, and race to avoid getting into trouble with the Federal Housing Administration (FHA),

Not Building a Team and Playing It Solo

As said earlier about building your real estate empire, you need a team. Even if you don't want to build a real estate empire, you can't handle multiple real estate properties alone. Trying to save money by playing it solo will kill you.

The stress and pressure of managing a rental real estate property are much more than one person can do.

The Kelvin Ortner said, "Owning a commercial or residential rental property can be both time-and capital-intensive. Trying to handle it all solo can require a level of focus and commitment that may not be realistic for every investor. A simple way to avoid that mistake is building a team from day one." Leverage a team to manage the property to avoid bearing all the stress alone. Don't make this mistake.

Not Knowing and Understanding the Market

You have to understand your market before you purchase real estate. This is true whether you are buying to rent or buying to sell. As a real estate investor, you don't make a profit by just holding the property. That's appreciation. However, the profit is made when you rent or sell the property. As a result, you need to understand the dynamics of the buying and selling market before you buy it.

Buying a real estate in an area where jobs are moving is a recipe for disaster. You are just going to lose money. That's the reason you have to listen to local, national, and international news before buying any real estate investment. If the government is going to demolish buildings in an area and you went ahead to buy a property there, you'll be in trouble.

Pay close attention to the market and get accurate information about the area before investing. An entrepreneur will do market research to know and understand his customer before producing a product. This increases the prospects of success. You need to do the same thing. Have a good understanding of rental and tenant conditions of the area before investing.

Getting Bad Advice That Ruins the Property

Nothing kills real estate like bad advice. Therefore, you need to be careful about the kind of advice you take in running your real estate properties. You have to learn to take advice, but carefully analyze them before acting on them. Listen to people, but follow your own judgment, decisions, and intuition. Don't just do something because someone told you to do it.

The biggest mistake many mistake real estate investors make is listening to their real estate broker or agent too much. They fail to do their own research and out of greed invests in a losing property that drains their cash flow and capital. Don't let this happen to you. Always make sure you have questioned, reviewed, and evaluated any advice carefully before taking actions.

CONCLUSION

The following book is reproduced below with the goal of providing information that is as accurate and reliable as possible. Regardless, purchasing this book can be seen as consent to the fact that both the publisher and the author of this book are in no way experts on the topics discussed within and that any recommendations or suggestions that are made herein are for entertainment purposes only. Professionals should be consulted as needed prior to undertaking any of the actions endorsed herein.

This declaration is deemed fair and valid by both the American Bar Association and the Committee of Publishers Association and is legally binding throughout the United States.

Furthermore, the transmission, duplication, or reproduction of any of the following work including specific information will be considered an illegal act irrespective of if it is done electronically or in print. This extends to creating a secondary or tertiary copy of the work or a recorded copy and is only allowed with express written consent from the Publisher. All additional right reserved.

The information in the following pages is broadly considered to be a truthful and accurate account of facts, and as such, any inattention, use, or misuse of the information in question by the reader will render any resulting actions solely under their purview. There are no scenarios in which the publisher or the original author of this work can be in any fashion deemed liable for any hardship or damages that may befall them after undertaking the information described herein.

Additionally, the information in the following pages is intended only for informational purposes and should thus be thought of as universal. As befitting its nature, it is presented without assurance regarding its prolonged validity or interim quality. Trademarks that are mentioned are done without written consent and can in no way be considered an endorsement from the trademark holder.

www.ingramcontent.com/pod-product-compliance
Lightning Source LLC
LaVergne TN
LVHW022311200926
848481LV00004B/1282

9781807650438